"A poignant, compelling, redemptive cry of the heart. Each of the thirty-four short chapters invites readers to slow down, to reread them before moving on. Like waves rolling in on an ocean seashore, each successive chapter immerses the reader in worlds of heartache and hope. The interplay of Reformed, Mennonite, Catholic, and Anglican voices is, in itself, a powerfully instructive case study in the formation of a contemporary disciple of Jesus. Yet that pales in comparison with the soulful lament of a son grappling with the memories and legacy of trauma. I found myself bracing against the author's noble candor, yet doubly grateful for the solemn invitation here to behold the fierceness of familial love and paradoxical splendor of divine redemption that contends with the wounds of a world gone wrong."

—JOHN D. WITVLIET
professor of worship, theology, and congregational and ministry studies at Calvin University and Calvin Theological Seminary

"The wrath of father figures—in our childhood homes, in our praying hearts—has been a pervasive, occupying force in our culture for too many generations. It might be coming to an end. Arthur Boers's tender new memoir leads the way for the next generation's work of repair, healing, and writing a better story together."

—CHRIS HOKE
director of Underground Ministries and author of *Wanted*

"Arthur Boers's memoir, *Shattered*, takes us on a pilgrimage through his life of shattered glass and grace. Boers invites us into his personal narrative of family and faith with ecumenical reverence and a storyteller's curiosity."

—SANDRA McCRACKEN
singer-songwriter and author of *Send Out Your Light*

"His father's business was greenhouses, and Arthur Boers's *Shattered* is a memoir haunted by glass. Glass breaks in his father's rages, yet it also illuminates and ultimately proves the truth of Boers's words that 'entering the world of trauma is like looking through fractured glass.' Boers's Dutch immigrant family brought a legacy of trauma to Canada from Nazi occupation and from customs in which 'Boers men beat Boers sons.' The author, a father himself and an Anglican priest, finally escapes his history. Ultimately, *Shattered* is a meditation on violence and family, redemption, and Eucharistic transformation. In an era as rightly concerned as ours about violence—collective, familial, natural, political—I can't imagine a more important story."

—S. PAOLA ANTONETTA
author of *The Terrible Unlikelihood of Our Being Here*
and *Make Me a Mother*

"Arthur Boers's memoir, *Shattered*, takes its title from his intimate knowledge of glass—as the son of a father who made greenhouses; as the son of a father who threw a potted geranium through a plate glass window when angered; and, finally, as a minister who 'stayed pressed against the glass' (as Simone Weil says in an epigraph to the book), looking for clarity, for the clear light of God. At the book's center is the question, How do I reconcile all I knew and felt about my father? But this is no memoir of blame. Wonderfully complex, Arthur's narrative crisscrosses Dutch history, his family's immigration to Canada, his Calvinist upbringing, and his search for a faith that includes joy, freedom, social justice, and theological rigor. Arthur's desire: to transform the jagged, shattered glass of imsmigrant frustration and alcohol-fueled rage into the smooth beauty of beach glass. And as Arthur's understanding of his father's and his father's father's contradictions grows more complex, he accomplishes just such a transformation—not by simplifying his father or by knowing him any better, but by accepting his father in all his manifestations. This book very carefully fixes the shattered glass of his childhood, replacing what's broken with new, reglazed glass from which he looks out on the world."

—ROBERT CORDING
author of *Without My Asking* and *Walking with Rudin*

SHATTERED

A Son Picks Up the Pieces of His Father's Rage

ARTHUR BOERS

WILLIAM B. EERDMANS PUBLISHING COMPANY
GRAND RAPIDS, MICHIGAN

Wm. B. Eerdmans Publishing Co.
4035 Park East Court SE, Grand Rapids, Michigan 49546
www.eerdmans.com

29 28 27 26 25 24 23   1 2 3 4 5 6 7

ISBN 978-0-8028-8246-2

Library of Congress Cataloging-in-Publication Data

A catalog record for this book is available from the Library of Congress.

Gratitude grows for

Rae Struthers,
my first intellectual mentor,
whose tender probing guidance
taught me to mark books,
and dig into my life,
with persistence and courage;

and
for the memories of

Henri Nouwen (d. 1996) and Eugene Peterson (d. 2018),
who,
in essential moments,
like other pastors in my life,
became as fathers to me.

. . . the lovely contradictory nature of glass . . . while it is as frail as the ice on a Parramatta puddle, it is stronger under compression than Sydney sandstone, . . . it is invisible, solid, in short, a joyous and paradoxical thing, as good a material as any to build a life from.

—Peter Carey
Oscar and Lucinda

Glass is brittle, which is one of its weaknesses, but . . . also enormously durable and flexible, and, in the creative hands of an experienced and knowledgeable craftsman, it is almost infinitely malleable.

—Alan Macfarlane and Gerry Martin
Glass: A World History

Will you have pity, O Light, and break the glass, at the end of this perpetual duration? Even if not—one must stay pressed against the glass.

—Simone Weil
The First and Last Notebooks

FOREWORD

Early in this deeply moving and wonderfully compelling memoir, Arthur Boers writes: "Can I ever understand?" He's referring here to "Calvinist fatalism" combined with a "Dutch matter-of-factness that discourages exploring feelings and regrets or listening to pain." Later, but still early in *Shattered*, comes this: "So much hostility, so much outrage, spewed in so many different directions. I hardly know what to make of it." And soon after comes, "How do I reconcile all that I know and feel about my father? What to make of the men in my world?" I point these out to you, dear fortunate reader, because they seem to me emblematic of the immensely sound artistic approach Arthur Boers has taken in the creation of this unforgettable memoir.

Too many memoirists, sadly, use the form as a sort of public therapy where the writer (and main character) sets out not so much to genuinely explore his or her own story but to air what the author already knows of it. Memoirs like these tend to lean toward self-pity or self-aggrandizement or both, and their ultimate aim lies in getting even with the villains of their youth. The effect on the reader is often not a soul-affirming illumination of shared human experience but one of diminishment, the kind one feels when witnessing an ugly family argument with no larger context through which to see and hear it.

But what is so remarkable about *Shattered: A Son Picks Up the Pieces of His Father's Rage*, is that quite the opposite happens here; instead of Arthur Boers simply setting out to show us his late father's disturbing acts of violence toward his only son, the author has written a memoir rooted in an authentic desire to make sense of it all, to uncover what needs to be uncovered, not as an exercise in mere exposure but as a sincere effort to plumb the complex depths of his relationship with his flawed father. The result of this more courageous artistic stance is that, as in life, there emerge here no black-and-white caricatures of human beings whatsoever. Instead, Boers's father, whom the author still clearly loves and who, it becomes clear, despite everything, loved his son, becomes wonderfully three-dimensional and alive and real on the page.

This subject matter alone is certainly worth a book-length's excavation, but *Shattered* is so much more than the ageless tale of a son and father and those frayed ties that don't always bind; it is also a fascinating examination of Dutch immigrant culture in Canada in the 1960s and 1970s; it is a riveting look at Glazen Stad, "Glass City," a region near Rotterdam on the coast of the North Sea where for over one hundred years the building of greenhouses has been a major industry; it is a beautifully written coming-of-age story, set so evocatively on the shores of Lake Ontario; but more than any of these, *Shattered* is the portrait of the writer and pastor as a blossoming young man, a love letter to his calling to the spiritual life: "I did not ask to long for God. Yet nothing draws me more, even now."

Yet this is not simply the impressive work of a pastor who can write really well. It is also a glorious expression of what Arthur Boers has also been for his entire adult life: a writer.

William James reminds us: "introspection is retrospection." And in his 1993 memoir, *This Boy's Life*, Tobias Wolff tells us, "Memory has its own story to tell." Meaning, of course, that each of our own memories is deeply subjective and ever evolving, and that while factual accuracy is desired, what is desired even more is a full rendering of the memoirist's memory of what she *believes* actually happened. At one point in *Shattered*, after describing a particularly painful moment at the hands of his father, Arthur Boers goes on to list the traits of all the other fathers in the neighborhood who were clearly far more abusive and-or neglectful than the author's father had ever been or would be. But Boers does this without trying to whitewash or excuse the elder Boers's behavior, but to simply put it into a context whose essence is suffused by the light of the author's own sincere and legitimate questions about his father's sometimes horrific behavior and his larger family's nonresponse to it.

And then there is all the *glass* that lies whole or in shards throughout this important work. Yes, there is "Glass City," and yes, the author's father made a living designing and building greenhouses as a Dutch immigrant in Canada, and yes, when the author was a boy he cut his hands many times working for his father, but if I have ever witnessed a more deeply rooted, organic, or convincing metaphor undergirding a novel or memoir, I cannot recall where or when. It is utterly successful and rings perfectly true, and it calls to mind the archaic opposite of the verb "to remember" being not "to forget" but "to dismember." In that sense, then, all of our memories are a reaching for the shards of past experience, a gathering of the fragments that may, in time, make a more meaningful and ultimately more restorative whole.

This is precisely what Arthur Boers has achieved in this superb memoir, and—I'm willing to bet—at no small cost to himself. This is one of those rare memoirs that is honest yet fair, that pulls no punches yet lands at a place of hard-earned light and repose. At one point, Boers writes, "I want to believe that brokenness is not the entire story, not even the end of the story." Well, in this author's sure hands, hands that bear scars of long-ago damage, I'm willing to believe he is more than right.

Andre Dubus III

ONE

"Ow, you're hurting me!" are among the first words I remember, an oft-repeated, all-too-familiar refrain. The complaint crept through the thin wall between their bedroom and mine, startled pain suddenly sparking from her tone then clanging in my ears.

I did not stay in bed or wish the sound away. I did not cover my head with my pillow to drown it out. I did not close my eyes, hoping to sleep. Instead, I felt called; I had a duty. I rose on the wobbly mattress, flannel giraffe pajamas damp from sweaty sleep, my hair mussed. I clambered over my crib rail, pivoted my torso across, and dropped to the hardwood. I ran, out my door and into theirs, arms stretched high, crying "Superman!" Bounding over the floor I leaped onto the double bed that almost filled their room. Crawling over bunched sheets and prickly woollen blankets, squirming between my mom and dad, I pried apart their grappling. I felt no danger to myself, but I wanted my mother safe.

They laughed at three-year-old me.

I don't laugh now.

He manhandled her, poked her ribs and belly, twisted arms, tested limits. My rush to intervene became a routine. Years passed before I realized their collusion. Sometimes they made early morning noise just to enjoy the pajama-clad toddler's rescue efforts. A great way to start the day, another hilarious family story. They meant no harm; they were just playing. Unable to distinguish protest from pretense, I joined their drama.

Yet she did not always pretend. This was not always a game. On occasion her tone rang pain-tinged, her voice rising: "Ow, you're hurting me!" Words twisted in excruciation. Failing to sort out aches from acting, I always reacted, certain I did the right thing.

1

Rescuers—shining-armor knights, steed-mounted cowboys, my name-sake King Arthur—deliver distressed damsels. Victims suffer a villain's dastardly deeds; Dudley Do-Right sets things straight. TV—*Tarzan, Robin Hood, The Lone Ranger*—taught me scripts that I enacted over and again, from my bedroom to theirs.

My father regularly went off course—drinking too much, smashing a car and forgetting how it happened, exploding with expletives. My mother would recruit another man in the family—her father or his uncle—to "talk to Pleun." Papa would straighten out for a time, but the reform never lasted. Eventually I would be tapped to intervene. No doubt that contributed to my formation later as a pastor, perpetually looking out to rescue others.

⇒⇐

In our small apartment on Martindale Road, I admired the Indonesian batik draped on the living room wall. Eventually I would learn that my father brought that back from his military service, a time measured in months that burdened him with forty-plus years of sweat-drenched nightmares. Below the colorful fabric squatted a gray couch; kitty-corner from the sofa was a matching chair. I ran toy cars along the upholstery, creating curving roads from the warp and weft, soft mountains out of armrests and cushions. Resting atop a shelf, a light brown starfish—knobbly and dried—leaned against the wall. For years I would assume it came from nearby Lake Ontario, where we occasionally went to the beach. A geranium in a clay pot, given by a local greenhouse farmer, sat on our pine coffee table, as did a stubby brown bottle of Old Vienna beer sweating beside it. A multicolored glass bowl was also on the table, often filled with McIntoshes; that bowl always on display, wherever we lived, until it and I were shattered on the same day. A wide ashtray collected my father's Buckingham butts, and a cigarette package, with royal looking gold-and-scarlet coat-of-arms, perched on the edge. Greenery sprouted on windowsills.

The potted geranium—leaves and flowers trembling—hurtled toward the picture window, moist dirt drifting down, sprinkling onto the carpet. I watched without surprise. I already knew that such things happened in our house.

My mother ducked. The pot passed her and struck the pane, the bump at first hardly audible. The surface gave slightly, shimmering and reverberating, a softly tinkling cymbal, then spidered suddenly in all directions.

Chiming splinters hailed down. Large shards wobbled and dropped, some impaled the floor inside and the lawn two floors down outside, others shattered as they fell to wood and earth. The plant continued its angry alfresco arc before abruptly plummeting from sight.

Once objects stopped moving and the pane ceased disintegrating, when no more glass fell, I heard robins in trees and cars passing a block away. Cool air, hinting of spring thaw, seeped around—scents I encountered often over the following years in many greenhouse visits.

I was there.

Only three, what could I understand? Glass breaks, I learned that early. But no one told me that smashing windows is outlandish—a troubling, dangerous infraction of civility, family life, simple good sense, thrift, safety.

I remember nothing about their argument, points scored, insults lodged. Picturing this now, I see my parents as I knew them later, middle-aged or older and certainly ought-to-know-better. Doing the math, I realize that she was twenty-seven and he thirty-three, both of them younger than my adult children. I could be the father of my troubled, immature parents.

At half my present age, my parents had already endured more trauma, danger, and loss than I will ever know. They witnessed lives taken by Nazis and feared their own apprehension, suffered the deprivations of economic collapse, weathered their own parents' violence, and gave up almost everything when they immigrated to Canada from the Netherlands. They were only allowed to bring one crate of belongings and $50 per person to this foreign country where they could not speak the language and were insulted as "DPs"* and told to "go back to where you came from." They knew about trying to survive, not the luxury of dwelling on feelings—their own or others'.

Over the years, my family talked about this incident with the pot of geraniums, and Papa never showed embarrassment or remorse about this or any other tantrum. Men did not have to explain, let alone apologize. In each recounting of the window breaking, both parents again and again

---

* *DPs*: Shortened form of "Displaced Persons," the name applied to the millions of European refugees or exiles after World War II—whether they were rendered homeless by the war in some way (for example, by battles or bombs) or by being imprisoned or enslaved by the Nazis. (Even after the Allied rescue, many DPs were housed in camps.) Dutch immigrants resented a label that felt like being called victims; they chose immigration and volunteered to leave their homes, worked to support themselves, and were not the objects of charity.

agreed on the most amusing aspect. As that plant hurtled past my mother, I taunted—inspired no doubt by the *Three Stooges*, a show my father and I enjoyed together—"Nya, nya. You missed her!" In some tellings I stuck out my tongue and blew a raspberry.

Whenever the memory of the shattered window came up, they always laughed and concluded with my wisecrack.

After his outbursts my father left others—my mother, employees, eventually my sister and me—to pick up literal and figurative pieces. Hurled objects were never his responsibility. Other people or circumstances were to blame for his rage. Someone else could make amends, as my mother often did.

This time too. Safety demanded that she clean up right away, carefully sweeping with dustpan and broom and then vacuuming finer fragments. She warned us to avoid the area near the window, especially in socks or bare feet. For months afterward, she found errant unexpected slivers, stuck in carpet fibers, randomly sparkling in the sunlight.

And reputation required that she get out to the yard soon, retrieving sharp shards, not to mention the smashed pot and broken plant. Quickly, so the neighbors did not see, did not know, did not figure out, that Pleun lost his temper—again.

I could not yet articulate what I was beginning to learn. Men explode dangerously. No one is safe around my dad. Be wary. Wiser to stay on the far side of the room. Sometime it might be me on the receiving end and— with practice—he would not miss.

⸺

I have always noticed glass, paid attention to it. One relative ate it, although not on purpose, badly damaging his intestines. My father used it in his work, repairing and building greenhouses. He bought it wholesale to sell to greenhouse farmers.

And when angry, he flung and smashed it.

At home, we stored and sold it. As a teenager, I unloaded, moved, and stacked bulky seventy-five-pound wooden crates, *kists* in Dutch, filled with glass panes—from manufacturers' transport trucks into our storage, or into customers' vans, or onto our pickups for delivery to construction sites. *Kist* is Dutch for "crate," "chest," or "box"; it can also mean "coffin" or "casket."

The cheap wood put splinters in my palms and blisters on my fingers. The work taxed my muscles and had to be done carefully. Unwieldy cases bore the label "Fragile Contents" and I wore steel boots to prevent my toes getting crushed.

All that damned glass.

⟹⟸

As an Anglican priest I intone at funerals, "Earth to earth, ashes to ashes." George Herbert, another Anglican priest, in his poem "Church Monuments," wrote that "flesh is but the glass, which holds the dust."* Glass is made from sand, a form of earth, and combined with ashes. Sometimes it forms naturally when lightning strikes beaches. Perhaps observing that long ago gave people the idea. Glass manufacturing goes back more than 5,000 years. Ancient Romans already had glass windows.

Glass is central to our lives. Windshields and windows, telescopes and test tubes, binoculars and bulbs and barometers, microscopes and mirrors and magnifiers, lights and lenses, preserving jars and prisms. Jewelry, vases, stained glass, chandeliers, crystal goblets. Glass improves vision for the short- and farsighted. With my first pair of glasses at age ten, green blotches above my head and below my feet resolved into discrete tree leaves and distinct grass blades, thousands and tens of thousands of them. I had no idea until then.

And glass sparks our imagination: Cinderella's slipper, Sleeping Beauty's *kist*, warnings against living or throwing stones in glass houses. We read *The Glass Castle*, *The Glass Menagerie*, *The Glass Key*, and of course, *Through the Looking Glass*. From TV I knew about glass eyes—often a villain's disfigurement—and in fights one hoped for the happy prospect of an enemy's glass chin. When I was a young adult, the band Blondie introduced a "heart of glass." The apostle Paul writes that "now, we see through a glass darkly." In Arthurian legends, my namesake disappeared into Avalon, the Isle of Glass, and Merlin was trapped in a glass house or glass cavern.

Glass connotes peril. The "broken windows" theory suggests that shattered panes adversely affect urban crime rates. As a teen I read of Novem-

---

* George Herbert, *George Herbert: The Country Parson, The Temple*, ed. John N. Wall Jr. (New York: Paulist Press, 1981), 181.

ber 1938 when Nazis attacked Jewish businesses, storefronts, homes, synagogues—an event called *Kristallnacht*, Night of Broken Glass, because of smashed panes littering streets and sidewalks.

On my far smaller scale, fractured glass felt personal. I learned wary attention.

Recently, searching for sea glass, I visited Port Weller's Jones Beach, at the fringe of St. Catharines, Ontario. For most of my life being near water has fascinated me, especially at the edges—coasts and riverbanks. For security or respite or escape or adventure, I am never quite sure. But usually, and preferably, in solitude and often for solace. The surface light, the murmur of water's movement, the rhythm of its waves, all speak to me of God and God's creation. The beauty draws me.

We moved near Jones Beach when I was four and away just before I turned twelve. Summer afternoons when I was eleven, I would walk a half mile to that crowded sandy stretch almost daily, except Sundays—we were Dutch Calvinists, and Sabbaths must be kept sacred, so no swimming permitted—until the day broken glass sliced open my thumb and I went to the emergency room for stitches.

I have lived many places since, but Lake Ontario's southern shore always feels familiar, connected as it is to my family's history. A few miles east of Jones Beach, we regularly visited my grandparents in Niagara-on-the-Lake and strolled a block from their house to a clay cliff that overlooked the water. Twenty miles west of Jones was the lakeside farm where my mother's family first lived in a horse barn after arriving in Canada. Stand at any of those spots on a clear day and you can see across twenty plus miles of glassy expanse to the skyline of the city where I now live—Toronto, with its distinctive CN Tower spinning-top-spindle and jutting skyscrapers, hazy gray silhouettes wavering up out of the horizon.

The beach had changed since my last visit fifty years ago. There were more trees, large ones now. And the *strand* was duller, rockier, no longer groomed. *Strand* is Dutch for "beach." Sparkling yellow sand long since disappeared. Along the wrack line, my feet encountered twigs, Tim Hortons cups, algae. I stepped carefully over marooned driftwood. Gulls wheeled above decaying fish tossed up by the surf. The refreshment stand, where I was never allowed to spend money, was gone.

I visited in May, too early to swim, and saw four wanderers. One pair walked a Doberman. The other paced over rocky terrain, heads down, metal detectors probing air a few inches from the ground, searching for treasures, for something more substantial than beach glass.

A permanent sign stood sentinel, warning that there is never a lifeguard here; people swim at their own risk. Jones Beach pollution levels have been dangerously high for such a long time that the local public health agency no longer bothers testing it.

I had not been back to this beach since that long ago broken glass sent me to the ER. Yet here I stood, over a half century later, looking north, recalling my first impression of this lake—another of my earliest memories. Not much solitude that time, certainly no solace. When I was three my folks took me to a Lake Ontario beach with Mom's best friend, Tante Joyce, and her three children. Mom brought a nylon laundry line rope, tying one end to a tall maple, and the other around my waist. Water sparkled seventy-five feet away; she worried I'd wander. She needn't have bothered. Robert, Joanie, and Howard cavorted but I stayed on the Dutch woollen blanket, petrified by the undulating blue. I did not yet know the consolation of abiding near water. This was not yet safe haven.

Fearful of the view, I sat in the shade and bawled, but I could not look away.

TWO

Sorting through baby photos I came across one that most would regard as happy. My grandmother apparently did. I am not as sure.

In the early years of my parents' marriage there was little or no work most winters. A few times water and phone services were disconnected. When I was born, they could not afford the doctor, a fellow church member. He badgered them for payment until my father blew up. When my mother became pregnant again, they went to a new doctor—unchurched, not Dutch—and she warned him that they had no money. He was unconcerned: "Pay when you can." My father learned from this. Thirty years after his death, his customers still appreciate how he built greenhouses on credit, letting farmers defer payments until crops came in.

In 1957, the year I was born, my father's house painting business failed. He settled debts and worked part-time driving a van on slushy St. Catharines streets, delivering newspaper bundles to corner stores and paperboys. This did not pay well. My mother's parents were always antagonistic toward my father, so my folks did not ask them for help. Instead Papa borrowed money to send my mother and me on a ship to stay with his parents in their Netherlands row house at Appelstraat 6 in Naaldwijk until finances improved.

My dad moved in with a generous Dutch immigrant family, the Sikkemas,* sharing their baby's nursery. They asked little for room and board, even when our collie, Prins, ate a hefty portion of their Christmas turkey. Mrs. Sikkema told me recently that my father "had big dreams, always" of becoming rich, hopes that seemed unlikely back then.

---

* Most names—apart from those of relatives—are changed to protect privacy. In any case, these are my perspectives, no one else's.

8

My parents planned a six-month separation; my mother lasted two. Relatives report I had a glorious time abroad. But my mother was homesick for her husband and Canada. She persuaded my father to let her return home early. He borrowed money for those tickets too.

Since I cannot recall my infant odyssey to my grandparents, my first memory of the Netherlands is as an eleven-year-old visiting my by-then-widowed grandmother in the Glazen Stad for a month. *Glazen Stad* means "Glass City," a Dutch region near the North Sea coast, not far from Rotterdam, where greenhouses have been a major industry for well over a century, cultivating grapes the size of North American plums; tulips, roses, and carnations shipped around the world; and all manner of vegetables—tomatoes, green beans, bell peppers, cucumbers. Hearing of the Glazen Stad as a child, I thought of Oz's Emerald City and Sunday sermons about "clear as glass" New Jerusalem.

Oma lived at the edge of Naaldwijk, in the last row of narrow townhouses, intriguingly resembling those I had seen on British TV shows. After ascending steep ladder-like stairs to stand in a second-floor bedroom, I saw through the window miles of greenhouse roofs: glass peaks zigzagging up and down, silvered symmetrical waves, crystal crests crossing to the horizon, miles and miles of gardens under glass.

My father and his family came from the Glazen Stad. My mother's parents were from another part of the Netherlands but also lived in the Glass City for a time—it's where they met. My dad's father sold supplies to greenhouse farmers, and later my dad's mother supplemented her widow's pension by expertly pruning hothouse grape bunches to produce fat round juicy globes. My father grew up surrounded by glass and then made his living by laying more of it around the world.

On Sundays, my grandmother and I walked along blocks of row houses to her Calvinist church.* A modern building, with large swaths of glass in its

---

* *Calvinism*: John Calvin was a leader of the Protestant Reformation, second in fame only to Martin Luther. Calvinism prevailed among Puritans in England and in America, Presbyterians in Scotland, and in Reformed churches in Hungary. This form of Protestantism grew so prevalent in the Netherlands that the main Reformed denomination became the state church. Calvinism emphasizes God's sovereignty, Old Testament covenant theology, predestination, theological rigor, and doctrinal purity. These priorities play out in valuing hard work and thrift, honoring the Sabbath by attending church twice on Sundays and abstaining from work and spending money on that day, ethical rigor and strict church discipline, maintaining austere lifestyles, singing Psalms in worship, and promoting Christian education.

walls and an interior filled with tall green plants, emulating local hothouses, a Glazen Stad tribute. Donors to that project no doubt were greenhouse farmers or greenhouse builders or greenhouse suppliers. Many glass-shaped lives.

During my visit as an eleven-year-old, relatives and friends alike told me how as a baby I joyfully rattled the bars of my playpen, bouncing on my toes whenever anyone approached. I stretched my arms high for someone to scoop me up. I liked the comfort of being held.

As the first and until then only grandchild, and named after Opa Arie to boot, I garnered lots of attention. My grandparents had seen little of my father, their only child, for years. After emigrating he had never been back to the Netherlands, and might never return as far as they knew, not even to visit. They seldom heard his voice. Transatlantic phone calls—expensive, inconvenient, echoes reverberating and colliding with each other down long tunnels—happened once or twice a year. I can only imagine how much the arrival of daughter-in-law and grandson meant to them. They lobbied my mother to stay permanently and asked my father to come back, offering to buy us a house. My parents declined.

⊒⊏

My grandfather, father, and I were seldom together on the same continent, much less the same room. But there is a photograph snapped in my grandparents' living room that is a kind of group shot. In this triptych, the three of us—grandfather, father, son—ascend diagonally in black and white. Arie Boers, my paternal grandfather, stands in his row house living room, in front of the rippled glass of a door, holding his infant grandson Arthur up to a photo of my father on the wall. We measure a direct line. Arie, the man holding me, was his father's oldest son. Arie's oldest son (and only child) was my father whom he named Pleun after his own father. And I, the baby in the middle, was Pleun's first, and at that point only, child. I would always be his only—I resist the adjective "begotten"—son. Pleun named me after his father just as Arie had done.

I remember that room well. I visited it several times over three decades. Mottled wallpaper and lingering fragrances of bitter coffee, overboiled tea, hazelnuts, milk chocolate—a combination of scents that I would always recognize even though years separated my stays there.

My grandfather wears a darkly sober suit as he normally did in photos. As men did in 1957. His silvery tie slightly loosened, almost informal.

Maybe it's Sunday afternoon, church obligations fulfilled. A plain wedding band, one that eventually migrated to my finger, glints from his right hand, the customary place for Dutch Protestants to proclaim marital status. He's fifty-four. I am over a decade older than that now, but to my eye today he could be seventy-something. I wonder whether I'll ever look his age.

Arie's short dark hair is plastered into a sparse comb-over, a large mole looming from his tonsure. His chin juts in concentration. His mouth slightly open, not quite smiling. Lifting me, his only grandchild so far, his hands cradle my rump. Arie's eyes, level with my little shoulders, gaze at my back.

My grandfather, like Abraham, offering me up as a sacrifice—not to God, but to my dad. Isaac seemed uneasy during that journey with his father. When I read between the Genesis lines it looks to me like he was damaged for life. I can relate.

≽≼

Nine-month-old me has more hair than Arie. I wear a T-shirt; chubby legs dangle beneath Opa's hands. As in another photo from that stay, I intently reach for something; here my left hand grips the framed photo hanging on the wall. My fingers disappear behind it, thumb pressing the glass.

I surely cannot recognize the photo's image of my Pa—as a child I called him Papa—and am just curiously grabbing; maybe Opa directed my attention. But the viewer wants the scene sentimental: baby reaching for father, the faraway man, on the other side of the Atlantic. The baby appears determined. No one seems worried I might tug the picture from the wall, knock it to the ground, shatter its glass. But I look like I would not hesitate.

≽≼

My grandmother, Oma, wrote on the back of the small black-and-white of this scene: *Zie zijn kleine duimpje op de foto van jouw.* "See his little thumb on the picture of you."

The "you," almost under my thumb, is her son, my father Pleun. Behind glass, dark hair slicked back, sheening from the photographer's flash. A formal head and chest shot: mid-twenties, in black suit and knotted tie, taken prior to his emigration. He kept trying to get away. Oddly, evergreen sprig antlers jut from the top of the frame.

His wire rimmed glasses and angular face incline toward his right, seemingly at the baby who may be trying to tug him from the wall, to take down his father. I face my dad's image, reach toward him—as I often did in life, seldom succeeding. Opa looks at me from behind. I am the center of attention in this potentially happy domestic scene.

The top of my head is three or four inches above Opa's, a couple of inches below my dad's crown. In this staircase of skulls, Opa's head is the largest, mine smaller, and my father's the smallest—like helium balloons diminishing in size as they drift up and into the distance.

How can one tell that all three of us knew, or would know, what it means to be beaten, battered by fathers? That two abused their sons? I say this reluctantly—we never named these realities, and somehow I knew we were not supposed to talk about such things.

How can one tell from this cheery living room snapshot that for the three of us, home could be a place of terror and pain at the hands of someone we might expect to protect us? How does one photo contain so many contradictions of love and loss, affection and resentment, fondness and danger?

What do I do with the deep sorrow I feel when I think of this photo?

＝＝

My father's portrait hung in my grandparents' living room for forty years, until my widowed grandmother's advanced dementia forced her into a locked nursing home ward. In a narrow silver frame and wide white matting, the picture's prominence on the wall demonstrated how families once honored deceased loved ones.

Pleun worked hard at leaving them, crossing the Mediterranean and Red and Arabian seas, the Indian and Atlantic Oceans, first volunteering as a soldier in Indonesia and then moving to Canada. He had reasons: to fight for his country, to search for a better life—and also he wanted to get away. Each time he departed—first for perilous overseas battles and then for prohibitively expensive transatlantic travel—parents and son never knew whether they would see each other again. Did my father, their only child, regret these separations? I suspect not. But his parents kept wanting him back, wanting him safe, wanting him near.

I imagine my grandparents worrying about their only child fighting in jungles and rice paddies. When he finally returned, relief at his safety did not offer them long-term consolation. He immigrated to Canada a few years later. I do not know whether he tried staying in touch. I never saw him write a letter. After my folks married (only Oma could afford to attend the wedding), my mom took responsibility for correspondence, saving postage by cramming weekly news on flimsy blue airmail forms.

⇒⇐

When my mother and I stayed with them, Opa and Oma made the best of their only chance to celebrate St. Nicholas with a descendant. They never before had a Christmas tree, whether from Dutch frugality or strict Calvinism I am unsure, but they acquired one during our stay and decorated it, borrowing sparkling glass ornaments and purchasing colored light bulbs. Hence the pine sprig antlers adorning the living room photo.

People say that my grandfather, once so stern with my dad, doted on me. And here's how I know.

Audiophile Opa splurged on a Dutch-manufactured Philips radio. He enshrined the monolith, an elaborate affair with multiple dials and polished wood, on its own shelf. Opa precisely adjusted dials, poised to capture elusive radio waves of classical music on favorite hard-to-tune stations. He forbade anyone from touching his venerated object. Even my finicky housekeeper grandmother did not dare dust it. Company avoided it too. Opa's rowdy brothers had to keep *pooten* ("paws") off, especially when drinking.

But he welcomed my curiosity. Baby Arthur could play with the device, not just admire it from afar. Opa allowed my sticky fingers on its shiny surface, messing with painstakingly positioned knobs. So people tell me. A nice enough story that would be a little hard to believe, possibly apocryphal, if not for black-and-white proof. Still another photo. There I am, round-headed and beaming, my right index finger stretched, like Michelangelo's Adam toward God, straining straight at dials.

Did my own father have comparable fun with that man, his dad? I doubt it.

⇒⇐

I cannot ask. Direct witnesses gone, I puzzle things out by inference.

I, the oldest son in a line of oldest sons, examine our family tree and know this: Boers men beat Boers sons. Great-grandfather Pleun beat his

13

eldest, Arie, my grandfather, who abused his son Pleun, my father. I was only seven and blacked out the first time Papa beat me. I was always vigilant, always fearful. I heard that my grandfather resented my father for not being a girl and that this ramped his rage. How can this be? Grieving Oma's stillbirths and miscarriages I understand, but punishing the only living child for such sorrows or blaming his gender?

Perhaps my grandparents still felt shamed by his untimely arrival a few weeks short of nine months after their wedding. That timing triggered a visit from church elders who wanted to know whether the relationship had been consummated before the ceremony. If so, the young parents would endure public shaming on Sunday before the congregation; their Calvinism was stern. My grandparents, though, convinced the authorities of good behavior and escaped church discipline. But still. I only speculate.

Here is something I know. Pa could not wait to leave.

Some parents divide labor and chores. His parents allocated discipline. Oma punished little things, however she defined that. Trying to protect my father, she explained, seemed safer than letting Opa discipline. She seldom threatened, "Wait until your father gets home." My Oma frequently slapped my father, and she wielded wooden spoon, wicked wicker *mattenklopper* ("rug beater"), or some other household device against his posterior, hands, head, or back. She worried that their only child might grow up "spoiled." Their family, like mine, like most Dutch families I knew, was preoccupied with "spoiling" children. This was not only about wrecking a child but also worrying about how *others* might view their child-raising. Yet how to define "spoiled"? My firm disciplinarian parents did not spare the rod, did not spare me. I may not be spoiled, but at times I feel ruined.

The things we do from fear.

Worried about Opa's rampages, she punished and fed and put my father to bed *before* his dad returned from work. But Opa dealt with "bigger things." Character issues or flaws? Sneakiness? Lying? Defiance? I'm unsure. More than once at the end of a day though, Opa, still wearing heavy work boots, kicked his boy—one of the few things my father told me about his upbringing. Maybe it's not strange that Papa would also eventually boot me with systematic fury.

Oma said Opa didn't know how to stop. My mother said the same thing about my father: he did not know how to stop. My dad, once on the receiving end, ultimately delivered too.

In spite of beatings, my father enjoyed misbehaving. He often told me that threats never deterred him. "I knew I was going to be punished, knew that would hurt, but did it anyway. I couldn't stop myself." That out-of-control theme again. He disliked rules. Playing Monopoly with friends, he smuggled in his own play money for an advantage. Later, as a businessman he was sued for stealing a patent and, based on what he told me, I know he was guilty.

I wonder how I turned out to be such a goody-goody, cautious about rules and obsessed with avoiding parental disapproval. Afraid of being hit and hopeful that perfection would keep me safe? Trying to ingratiate myself?

⇉⇇

In the photo I am always struck by the presence of glass.

Biggest and most obvious is the pane behind my grandfather, in a door leading to a damp unheated front hall. All Opa's and Oma's inside doors resembled this one, two-thirds wood and a third translucent pebbled glass, typical in Dutch houses. You cannot see much through them, only distorted silhouettes. Privacy was never absolute, only partial. Light from the other side passes through, but no clear images. Such doors save energy, one room's illumination spilling into another, and contribute an illusion of spaciousness.

Glass on my father's photo is less obvious except for the slight camera flash sparkle. His framed picture resembles another window, this one above eye-level. We look up towards him, as though he regards us from the other side of the wall, perhaps gazing from a window on a higher plane, maybe the attic, not the other side of the ocean. But definitely behind glass.

Now at an age that neither of them ever reached, I have questions about them. About their relationship to each other and to me. About the anger and violence, the hydraulic fury, pulsating from generation to generation. The sins of the fathers, you might say. Sounds biblical. Mysteries to me, to each other, to themselves. But then perhaps not such a mystery after all. Angry abusive men appear throughout my family tree.

Such were the fathers I knew best.

THREE

Small signs suspended from barbed wire—battered, bilingual, bullet-holed—bore the same heading:

Department of National Defense
DANGER

One continued:

Firing Range
Keep Out

And the other, more ominously:

Military Target Area Zone
Do Not Touch Anything
It May Explode
And Kill You

After learning to read in first grade, I studied these backyard threats behind my maternal grandparents' two-bedroom bungalow in Ontario.

Across that fence, a forest stretched south and north, a hundred feet deep, crowded with tall oaks, littered with acorns. I never entered, but I stood at the edge and peered through barbed wire into the gloom. No one raked the accumulating leaves; little grew on the ground. I wondered about bears and wolves, picturing Little Red Riding Hood and Hansel and Gretel wandering in shadows. I never saw wildlife other than blue jays swooping from branch to branch, their emphatic calls punctuating the air, and the gymnastic antics of black squirrels, chattering and scolding, whether at each other or me, I never knew.

On days when flags went up at the Military Target Area on the other side of the trees, we heard the percussion of gunfire. Did my grandparents flash back to the invasion, occupation, and liberation of the Netherlands? Did they ever feel safe?

Their Shakespeare Avenue white clapboard, nestled in Niagara-on-the-Lake, was ten miles from our home. We saw them once or twice a week, at their place or ours or in church. I never knew Oma well. She died at sixty-five, when I was eleven, but I spent a lot of time with Opa and his youngest—two men who scared me more than the Department of National Defense signs.

———

Of all my relatives, I most resemble Herman, my mother's youngest brother. We are the only ones to pursue higher education, and both of us eventually became book-writing professors—he a historian specializing in Dutch immigration to Canada.

When I was a young teen he lived nearby for a couple years while writing his doctoral dissertation, and he took me under his wing. We argued theology and politics. His socialism shocked me, raised as I was by parents who feared that anything politically left could be a gateway for communism. We both loved history, and he took me to War of 1812 historical sites. We went smelt fishing at the Queenston dock, downstream from Niagara Falls, and discussed *Patton*, *Lawrence of Arabia*, and *Seven Brides for Seven Brothers*—a musical he and his wife loved.

Later he perplexed us. In his late thirties, he abandoned his wife and young children for an affair with one of his university students, a woman he went on to marry. He then spurned his family, refusing any contact. Even when his sons wed, when they became fathers and he a grandfather, he remained cut off—no cards or calls—rebuffing attempts to connect.

My parents appointed twenty-seven-year-old me—the responsible oldest grandchild—to phone when Herman's father, my grandfather, lay dying. Opa's last wish was to see his youngest once more. They had not been in the same room for years. I sat in my father's den for the call, looking out at my parents' suburban street and a Big Wheel in a neighboring driveway, and pleaded with Herman. He stonewalled, claiming he could not afford the trip all the way from Alberta. We offered to pay but to no avail. A month later Opa died and I phoned from that same room. We hoped Herman would attend the funeral but he declined, again claiming poverty and again refusing our offers of subsidy. When Herman was dying, thirty years later, no one told his sons. They learned of his death only when the second wife, the erstwhile university student, left a message on the eldest's machine.

Two things that Herman said haunt me—the first he said about me and the second about his relationship with his father.

When I was fourteen, my Dutch uncle, smart, sarcastic, master of insults and put-downs, called me an "automaton."

"Whadda ya mean?"

"You're too worried about what your parents think. You don't know who you are or how to be happy. You just do what they want."

That barb festered. Who knows how often I have been criticized over the years and how many insults I have forgiven or forgotten? But not this one. At some level I feared possible truth. I argued with him then, and in my mind often since, about this toxic observation.

In his second revelation, by then in his sixties, he threatened to write a book about his terrible father. I never knew his specific complaints. Opa was violent with my mother and presumably with Herman. Still, the long bitterness astonished me. Now in my sixties, I ponder my own late life father preoccupations. Another way I resemble Herman.

And I wonder: What did Opa do?

＞＝＜

In the 1920s, my mother's father, Jelle, was a young agricultural apprentice who ventured to the Glazen Stad from the northern province of Friesland to work in greenhouses. There, probably at church, he met Margje Timmerman. She had moved to the area to train as a nurse in a mental asylum, coming from the eastern province of Drente.

Margje found nursing too stressful and had a "breakdown; her nerves couldn't take it," I was told as a child by my mother. She ended up working in the hospital laundry instead. That disappointment—her *zwakke zenuwen*, "weak nerves"—haunted her.

The Glazen Stad shaped my grandfather's life another way, not just in finding a spouse. He worked among peaches grown in greenhouses, the Dutch climate too cold and damp for outdoor orchards. A hailstorm swept through, pounding glass into smithereens. Opa, underfed in his boarding house and always hungry, gleaned and ate some of the damaged fruit from the ground, unaware that granulated glass was hidden in the sweet softness. In the years that followed, he had several surgeries because of the internal damage—but none solved his digestive issues. In middle age, still suffering stomach problems, he brought his family to Canada. It was 1948. My mother was fourteen at the time. No more school for her; she had to work. They saved a year for a $1,000 down payment toward his surgery. A kind doctor operated, willing to wait for the balance of his fee. During Opa's months-long recuperation, my teenage mother was the family breadwinner, earning $17.50 for fifty-hour weeks assembling baskets at a factory in Grimsby. My grandfather's intestines were repaired, but his belly ever after bore scars, long crimson rifts, from all the interventions.

The Glazen Stad marked him as it marked us all.

⇒≡⇐

He wed Margje Timmerman and they settled in Friesland, where he managed greenhouses in a *proeftuin*, an experimental farm. Life was demanding, harsh.

Their first child, Meinderd, a son, was born during the Depression but died at a year and a half of an enlarged heart. Oma was pregnant with my mother at the time and had another emotional breakdown. My mother, Roelofje, only learned about the lost child and breakdown years after Oma and Opa died; such realities were not discussed. After my mother came her next brother, also christened Meinderd (it was a common tradition to name succeeding children after dead siblings) and, finally, Herman, midway through the German occupation, in 1942.

Many went hungry then, especially during the war's last year, the "Hunger Winter" of 1944–45. People, especially in the cities, ate tulip bulbs and longingly eyed neighborhood cats and dogs. But the Ganzevoorts lived in a rural area and Opa, a wheeler-dealer, bartered for food. After the Nazis left, he was accused of black marketing and jailed for a few days. Opa had gardens and access to local farms, but even he could not provide well-balanced diets. Insufficient vitamin C caused my mother to have scurvy, a term I encountered in grade school when I read of early sailors and explorers who spent months on ships.

There were other hazards.

A German deserter was rumored to be hiding in a nearby forest. One day, Opa, roaring his motorcycle down a road felt something brush his scalp. Stopping, he saw that a wire had been stretched across the road, presumably by the deserter trying to decapitate and rob a passing motorcyclist. Opa survived that trap because of his short stature, standing barely over five feet.

My mother recalls Opa's Resistance involvement. He would get a phone call and head off on mysterious nighttime errands, perhaps to hide Jews or transport downed Allied airmen. She loved standing in the shed and running her fingers through tall burlap bags filled with dried beans but one day was startled to pull out a sheaf of ration cards that must have been forged or stolen from the Nazis in an armed robbery. Knowing that their possession could mean arrest or worse, she hastily shoved them back, deep into the legumes. Near the end of the war, fearing Nazi reprisals, Opa went into hiding, sleeping elsewhere at night for several weeks.

After the war, in 1947, emigrants began leaving the Netherlands, including two ships destined for Canada.* Opa was forty-five when he and his family departed on a boat in 1948. The pace of immigration accelerated in the early 1950s. By then the Dutch government was paying people to leave.**

---

* *Reasons for immigration*: After the War, the economy was in shambles and unemployment high. Many buildings had been destroyed, making life difficult and causing housing shortages. Departing Nazis flooded five hundred thousand acres of farmland, so there were fewer places for farm laborers to work. With fresh memories of the occupation, many Dutch people feared that the Soviet Union would soon continue its march westward and the Netherlands would fall again. Also, a number of Dutch people were frustrated by their country's increasing bureaucracy and red tape (which made it difficult to get permits for rebuilding), despising the gradual drift toward socialism.

** *Choosing Canada*: The Dutch viewed Canada favorably. There Dutch Princess Juliana (in exile from the Nazi occupation) gave birth to Princess Margriet. Canadian soldiers were prominent in Holland's liberation. Canada needed agricultural workers and farm positions were in short supply in Holland. Meanwhile, Canada's immigration policies were biased in favor of white northern Europeans. Between 1947 and 1970, 185,000 Dutch immigrants came to Canada, about half of

I was born a dozen years after the Second World War, but my family's memories were fresh. The war continued to loom in the many stories they told. My mother remembers being a six-year-old and seeing German soldiers arrive on wobbling bicycles and trotting horses. For the rest of the war she and her friend Jitske never dared look down that particular road again, fearing further invasions. When Canadian soldiers drove out the Nazis, she heard artillery and gunshots. A neighbor, curious about battles between Allies and departing Germans, peeked his head around a hedge to look and was killed by a sniper.

A few years earlier another neighbor was suspected of butchering and selling meat on the black market. Nazis arrived one evening to arrest him. In the ensuing chase they all ended up in my mother's garden where soldiers fired weapons. In the morning my mom saw blood spattered on her tomato plants.

She and I visited Friesland fifty years later. As we drove on a highway, she spotted isolated farms in the distance and remarked, "That would have been a good place to hide. You could see for miles if Germans were coming." She spoke of fellow pupils who came to her Christian grade school with mysterious dark-haired "cousins from the city." After the war, she realized they had been Jews. She often told me that Calvinists and Catholics were the Christians who most consistently opposed and resisted Nazism.

War was not the only hazard. When my mother was twelve her mother beat a wooden shoe against her skull for not properly tending Herman in his carriage. A few years later her parents called her *hoer*, "whore," when she had her hair cut to have bangs. Several weeks before my parents married, she came in a few minutes after her 10 p.m. curfew and Opa slapped her, insulting her again with the outlandish accusation. Her fiancé, Pleun, threatened to strike them in retaliation. A few months later she fled the abusive household and married her volatile would-be rescuer.

---

them in the decade following the end of World War II. Herman Ganzevoort, *A Bittersweet Land: The Dutch Experience in Canada, 1890–1970* (Toronto: McClelland and Stewart, 1988), 72.

Depression, occupation, immigration. Miscarriages, mental illness, children's deaths, family abuse. Was anyone ever safe?

Combine such hardships with Calvinist fatalism about suffering and loss and a Dutch matter-of-factness that discourages exploring feelings and regrets or listening to pain. My ancestors concentrated on surviving, getting by. Little felt certain. Can I ever understand?

Here is a story that perplexes me. When a cousin fell, ripped his jeans and got a suture-worthy slice in his knee, his Dutch immigrant mother did not bring him to the hospital but scolded: "What's wrong with you? Knees heal, but jeans are expensive. They don't fix themselves." My cousin—he's around my age—still laughs as he tells this, not bothered. I always feel sad.

⇒⇐

How much of my grandfather's orneriness was cultural or contextual?

When grandfather Jelle Ganzevoort retired from landscaping he became a handyman in my father's business. He argued every day. With my father about petty cash. With my mother about where he could park in the yard. With other employees about sweeping the workshop or the Toronto Maple Leafs' prospects. With customers about weather predictions or corrupt politicians. With anyone about the world being flat and the moon landing being staged.

Behind his back, my parents called him "*Ouwe Jelle.*" *Ouwe* means "old" and *Jelle* is pronounced "yella," reminding me of the Disney tragedy *Old Yeller.* His thick accent barked and scolded. He snapped if restaurant wait staff offered salad. "Yech! I'm not a rabbit!" I only remember him silent when in church, which he tolerated, or while fishing, which he loved.

One Christmas our family and Oom Meinderd, his wife Tante Els, and their daughters gathered at Shakespeare Avenue for presents and a festive meal, as we always did. Opa unwrapped a gift. Tante Els, in her late twenties, leaned forward eagerly, "I found this just for you." He studied the elaborate fishing reel and responded, "Can I exchange it?" Els surged from the couch and bolted from the room, crying. Oma scolded Opa in Dutch. Later in the dining room we ate our lavish turkey dinner and no one spoke. Opa savored and smacked loudly—he always claimed a drumstick for himself—never indicating regret. When we got home, I asked my mother the meaning of "exchange."

Opa fought with his only brother. They so looked and sounded alike, one might think them twins. No one knows what tore them apart. Perhaps war tensions. Opa's brother may have been a Dutch Nazi, despised for collaborating with invaders. Maybe one asked for help and the other did not come through.

Or perhaps they got caught up in rancorous theological controversies. Their denomination split during the war.* Anxieties heightened by the war drove the intensity of such conflicts, much as the recent Covid-19 pandemic ratcheted up political North American hyperpartisanship. In Holland, even as people dealt with occupying invaders, now family members not only attended different churches, they would not speak to or visit each other.

Between 1948 when my grandfather left Holland and 1984 when he died, Jelle and his brother never once communicated. Like Herman, they could hammerlock a grudge.

≡≡

My parents commented that Jelle drove "like Jehu," the Bible's murdering charioteer. He raced his oversized four-door, eight-cylinder sedan down roads, his head barely showing above the steering wheel, with no regard

* *Dutch Calvinist Divisions*: Late in the war my grandparents' denomination deposed a minister over his views on the eternal status of unbaptized babies. This led to controversy over polity and how to address theological difficulties. A large group seceded to start a new denomination. They were called "Article 31" (referring to differences over polity) and named themselves *Vrijgemaakte*, "liberated"—loaded terminology when living under an oppressive occupation. Decades later, the divided denominations decided they believed the same on the question of common grace and unbaptized babies, but it was too late to reunite.

When I was growing up, relatives visited from the Netherlands every year, but one family declined our invitations because they would have to sit at our table when one of us non-*Vrijgemaakte* prayed over the food. I attended a Boers family reunion in the Netherlands in 1987. As the only minister in the extended family I was asked to preside over Sunday worship. My Article 31 relatives threatened to boycott the service, uncertain about my orthodoxy. I was a Mennonite pastoring a United Methodist church. But the liberated relatives informally interviewed me, were satisfied with my theology, and agreed to worship with the rest of the family. One great aunt, however, sat at the front, visible to all, and did not listen as I preached; instead she read her Psalter the whole time.

for speed limits. His homemade plywood trailer bounced behind his car, jostling lawn mowers, rakes, spades, gas containers, bags of fertilizer, and pesticides.

If a rabbit or pheasant ventured from a ditch near the shoulder, Opa veered his car, aiming. Bringing the trophy to our house, the do-it-yourself roadkiller butchered the prize out back and then asked my mother to cook it. He loved his meat rare and bleeding. His dentures gnawed and fretted at bones, carnivory that unsettled me.

When I was thirteen, he and I went to the Toronto airport to pick up my parents from a vacation they took after my father's first heart attack. A blizzard set in. In the middle of three lanes, barely able to see ten feet beyond the windshield, Opa accelerated and plunged the car into a whiteout between snowplows in the left and right lanes. And I felt terror.

⇒⇐

Still, I marvel at his resourcefulness—feeding his family during the war, participating in the underground Resistance, immigrating in his mid-forties.

In Canada, Opa worked for farmers and began a sideline selling used cars. That is how my father met him. Upon arrival in Canada, my dad went to a dealer and purchased a clunker not noticing that it had four different wheels. Church members told him about Jelle's used cars and he went to inquire at the Ganzevoort house. My mother happened to be at the window. "Look at that funny fellow, he's not wearing socks in his shoes," she mocked to her mother, who responded: "Be careful, next thing you know you'll be in bed with that man."

My father was content with the car that Jelle sold him, but many immigrants were not. Opa's reputation was sketchy and people confronted him about auto bargains that were anything but, scandalously bringing arguments even into the church parking lot before and after worship.

⇒⇐

When he turned seventy-one, I wished him happy birthday. He was operating a drill press in my father's workshop and grinned, noting that 71 is the reverse of 17, my age then. I was surprised—still am—that he noticed that sentimental detail. He then challenged me to a footrace on the driveway. I declined—he, still strong and lean from decades of labor, would probably have won.

He always competed.

When my mother and uncles were little, he strove to be the first to wish *Prettige Kerstfeest* ("Merry Christmas") or *Gelukkig Nieuwjaar* ("Happy New Year"), never allowing his children even that small triumph.

The April after I turned twenty-seven, Opa, a few months shy of eighty-one, was hospitalized in the Niagara-on-the-Lake hospital, where my sister had died a few years earlier. I lived in Chicago and took a week off work to visit. Mornings I birdwatched along Lake Ontario, trespassing on the Military Target Area, a half mile from his old house, stealing Department of National Defense warning signs. Afternoons I spent with him.

I told him that my wife, Lorna, was pregnant and he would be a great-grandfather in November. He said I should sell his car and save the money for his first great-grandchild, whether boy or girl.

He asked about my birdwatching, and I told him of an eastern belted kingfisher swooping from one dead branch overhanging the water to another. He argued, "There's no such bird. But in Florida I caught kingfish." Even my *Peterson's Bird Guide* did not persuade him. By the end of the week, he changed his mind and told me he'd been mistaken. Kingfishers existed after all.

This is the only time in my life that I remember a grown-up relative apologizing to me. To anyone.

FOUR

For three years after my mother and I traveled to the Netherlands, our family lived on Martindale Road, in a small two-bedroom apartment over a large double garage that contained a washing machine, laundry tubs, and clotheslines. My father stored his truck, cans of paint, and glass-filled *kists* there too.

When I was four, I regularly walked next door to see the Boot family, also Dutch immigrants, in their one-and-a-half-story house packed with boys. Their son Robby and I found an empty suitcase in a crawl space, and he obligingly folded himself to fit into it. His older brothers and I latched it but could not unsnap the catch and soon heard his muffled calls to be released. We hollered for Mrs. Boot. I was glad that it was him, not me, in there. The idea of such claustrophobic confinement still clenches my groin.

He and I bounced an Indian rubber lacrosse ball on the landing. "Be careful," Mrs. Boot called from downstairs, just as I let go of the heavy sphere. It smacked against a tall mirror leaning against the wall. Shattered pieces cascaded, littering the beige linoleum. "That's seven years bad luck," Robby intoned. I had no idea what he meant but was relieved that Mrs. Boot's only reaction was to send me home.

She often sent me home.

Robby, my age, wore thick-lensed spectacles. "Gimme your glasses, Robby." We were on the living room floor in front of the TV, taking in black-and-white cartoons.

"Naaah, I wanna watch Bugs Bunny."

"Just let me try 'em," I badgered.

Relenting, he handed them to me, and I settled them on my nose and swung my head. TV images and Robby and trees outside the picture window twisted and distorted, shrank, and then stretched. The blurriness surprised me.

"Give 'em back."

"In a sec."

"Now," his arm snaking my way.

I stood, pulled them from my face, and sprinted. Robby, sight impaired, stumbled after me. Then I pitched over a hassock, its corner jabbing my stomach and winding me. I rolled onto the ground, the glasses leapt from my hand, smacking down hard. A temple snapped and a lens fractured, zig zag lines erratically etching glass.

Mrs. Boot stepped into the living room. "Artur!"

"*Ongeluk!*" I yelled, hoping "accident" absolved me from a spanking or some other blow.

"I think you should go home."

Buying glasses was not in the Boot budget or ours. Bills for rent, electricity, groceries, and phone were challenging enough. My parents paid for a new pair. A few months later I could not resist temptation and snagged the spectacles from Robby's face, wanting to try them again, and ending with the same costly consequence.

＝＝

Our family spent frequent Sunday afternoons with the Vandenberg clan. Their farm, orchards and greenhouses, was outside the small town of Fruitland. Mr. Vandenberg—Oom Piet—and my father both came from Naaldwijk, had both volunteered as soldiers to keep Indonesia a colony, and were both proudly ornery political right-wingers.

His eldest was around my age, Dorothy, a Dutch girl cliché: Delft-blue eyes and blond hair held back by bright orange barrettes. I loved her frequent laughter and how she sat close to snuggle and warmly kiss us each hello and goodbye. She and I did a lot of imagining. She enacted Maid Marian to my Robin Hood, Jane to my Tarzan. Holding hands, we ran between low rows of McIntosh trees. We played house on the wide front porch; she heated tea and cooked while I went to work and came back to put up my feet. When not roaming or imagining outside, we got out Snakes and Ladders or creased card decks for War, or Go Fish, or *Peste* (a Dutch board game),* slapping cards down on their large wooden kitchen table. In the evening our two families crowded into their small living room and watched *The Wonderful World of Disney*; a few years later they became the first family we knew to acquire a color TV.

One day, clad in rubber boots, we came across cold frames in front of the orchard—*platte glas*, "flat glass," in Dutch. Her father had jerry-rigged these to give a head start to tomato plants. He'd hammered scrap wood planks into rectangles and laid old windows across, irresistible targets for neighborhood kids with rocks. Few remained intact. Dorothy and I waded through frames, avoiding jagged fragments jutting from the sides, breaking brittle ice-like surfaces with our boots, and moving to the next rectangle. Predictably, a piece stabbed my knee, and blood spurted. At the farmhouse Dorothy's mother sat me on the edge of their claw-foot tub to wash and dry the knee before bandaging it. No stitches for me. Medical care cost money. Extra expenses meant judgment calls.

I dreamed of snuggling always into Dorothy's safely reassuring affection. With my emerging English (we only spoke Dutch at home), I asked the obvious question: "Will you be my marry?" I imagined our secure life together.

Her "no" shocked me, then, even more when crying did not budge her.

I wondered what was wrong with me, caught off guard by a relationship not as safe and predictable as I supposed.

* *Peste* means to badger, nag, tease, spite, bully.

FIVE

As small children, my sister Margaret and I recited rote Dutch prayers before and after meals and when we lay down in bed. We learned them from my mother, who taught religion in our family. In spite of the famous hymn title, I absorbed the "faith of our mothers," or at least of my mother. Fathers were not so reliable. Mine attended church but was not expressive about faith. Before their wedding, my mother wrote out the Lord's Prayer for him to recite with the congregation during the service. That he did not know it astonishes me. He heard it every Sunday.

After supper we remained at our green metal table and Mom read the Children's Bible in her Dutch accent—"th" as "d," "v" like "f," "z" became "s"—her voice, to my mind, perfectly modulating the text. Papa tried to distract us, crossing his eyes, jutting his false teeth. I mostly ignored him because Bible adventures impressed me. I imagined them over and over. When Egyptians chased Jews through the Red Sea, I visualized *Jetson* robots with glowing lightbulb eyes, "Isra-*lights*," fleeing down tunnels. Believing in God was an adventure, but it also finally meant rescue.

⇛⇚

At age four I attended our church's Vacation Bible School (VBS), taught by blond Mrs. L, mother of five. I envied her family. They occupied the front pew on Sundays. Later as a teen I learned from my mother that Mrs. L "had to get married." She and Mr. L confessed before the church and then sat on hard wooden chairs for several weeks near the pulpit until the elders deemed their repentance properly fulfilled.*

Before my mother told me about Mr. and Mrs. L's unworthiness, one of Mrs. L's daughters and I went on a date to see *Murder on the Orient Express*. The following weeks I daydreamed during classes, entwining Janet's initials with mine in a notebook's margins. But each time I phoned and invited her for another outing, she claimed prior commitments. After half a dozen declined requests I realized that I would not sit with her again in my father's borrowed pickup, and certainly never at the front in church.

But as a child in VBS I admired Mrs. L, my first formal instructor. For years, every Sunday at church I called out when I saw her, "Hello, Teacher!" until she told me not to do that anymore.

I kept the VBS handouts that week, careful not to crease them, especially happy with the last day's showing Jesus on a cross, for our sins I'd been told. This illustration was rare. Calvinists, my mother said, opposed "graven images," pictures or statues.**

After the final VBS day I found my mother, the first theologian in my life, hanging wet laundry outside, her forearm muscles bulging under damp

* *Worm theology*: One of the few adornments in our church were Paul's words carved into the chest for storing offerings: "God loves a cheerful giver." I do not recall much cheerfulness, however. I often heard Psalm 22:6 (RSV): "I am a worm, and no man; scorned by men, and despised by the people." The Calvinism I experienced had a dour outlook on humans. The only people who were saved were those God chose, predestined, as part of God's covenant. Most people in history would not be so fortunate.

We were not as severe as some Calvinists. One group—the Free Reformed—preceded each Lord's Supper with a sermon reminding people of their unworthiness and depravity. Few if any dared to receive bread and wine; some members took communion only every few years; some never at all: "Wherefore whosoever shall eat this bread and drink this cup of the Lord, unworthily, shall be guilty of the body and blood of the Lord. . . . For he that eateth and drinketh unworthily, eateth and drinketh damnation to himself, not discerning the Lord's body" (1 Cor. 11:27, 29, KJV). Sometimes in those churches the elements remained on the table, untouched by anyone.

** *Calvinist iconoclasm*: God must not be portrayed; material things must not be exalted. Pious films only showed Jesus as a shadow; in *Ben-Hur* viewers saw him from behind or at a distance, never his face, only others' responses to him. As a young adult, I toured Europe and saw many pedestals, the consequence of Reformer acts of iconoclasm, often all that remained of "idolatrous" statues. In a small country church in Friesland, the top of the former altar lay as a threshold of the main door, so that dirty feet could be wiped on an idolatrous vestige.

sheets. I held up the image of three crosses with bearded and twisted occupants and asked, "Can I hang this in my bedroom?" I seldom dared anything without permission.

She helped me pin the pamphlet above my bed. I felt relief that my badness was solved. That night, and many nights after, I studied the tri-folded page, suspended like a butterfly, and murmured, "Thank you, Jesus," before tipping my face to the ceiling.

⇒⇐

My parents, conservative about much—no spending money or swimming on Sundays—liberally had Roman Catholic friends. Catholics might even end up in heaven, Mom told me, where eternity would give ample time for correction, for them to learn the truth.

She said "good Catholics" had wrong beliefs but could be generous, good-hearted. Once my parents visited a Dutch Catholic family, greenhouse customers of my father. That entire visit Margaret and I romped outside with their children's red wagon, on the gravel beside the boiler room. At the end of our time, Mrs. Van Noort told us, "You take that wagon home. We have two and only need one."

It was hard to keep all this information straight. Were Catholics good or bad? To be emulated or avoided?

Visiting a Catholic friend, Tante Corrie, in Owen Sound for a weekend, my mother and I attended Mass with her at St. Mary's of the Assumption. I wore a sports jacket and clip-on tie. My blond hair Brylcreemed, cowlick poking upward. I liked that—it reminded me of Dennis the Menace's unruly tuft.

People moved more quietly in that church than ours. Men in suits removed fedoras at the door. Women in dresses had solid dark lines running down the backs of their nylons.

Shadows lurked in corners. Candles sputtered on sloping tables. Nose tickling smoke drifted through the air. Pillars stretched high. Stained glass strained distorted light. I tried to stand on my seat to look at the movement, robes, personnel. So much to see and consider. But when I lifted my polished black shoes to the pew, hoping to stand on it, my mother swatted me. I slid forward, hooking my knees over the edge, dangling my calves, stretching my neck.

31

Tante Corrie, white lace pinned atop her dark hair, exited our bench, dipped a knee, folded her hands, and followed a slow-moving line to the front where a robed man dropped something small and white—a peppermint?—on her tongue. My mother told me that we were not permitted there.

I studied the statues: draped figures, some in white, others in blue, holding children, carrying books, clenching hands, gentle and friendly, sad and in pain. Gaudily wounded hands and sides, red beating hearts. My mother explained, "Catholics break the commandments. They pray to idols."

But wherever I turned, there he was, held by a mother, admired by adults, laughing and flinging arms, chubby and crowned, enthroned with a lady. "Ohhhh," I said, voice subdued. This was church and I was to be seen and not heard. "Look at all the Baby Jesuses."

SIX

Margaret and I had balloons, a rare treat. Hers was red and mine blue. We walked side by side through the living room, the flimsy spheres bouncing from strands of wool. My father, smoking in his chair, a Manhattan in his left hand, calmly reached over with his right hand, prodding first my balloon and then hers with the cigarette's glowing tip, laughing as balloons popped. Both of us started, and then cried.

A few months later, we had balloons again, this time passing as he drank coffee at the dining room table. He used a pointed pencil, with the same results and reactions, his and ours.

Another reason to stay away from him, on the other side of the room.

⇒⇐

I would never have been allowed to say what I think now: "I want to understand the things he did."

"Don't say 'want,'" Papa told me plenty of times. "It's rude."

And always with heat and exasperation, "Don't call grown-ups 'he' or 'she.' They're not dogs. Use their proper names. Be respectful." It was hard to distinguish respect and fear. My father played rough.

⇒⇐

He once tussled with his cousin, Art, who was around five then. My dad, twenty years older, had just arrived in Canada and was staying with his aunt and uncle in a small house on a farm near Lake Ontario. While wrestling, he yanked Art's ear and it partially detached, requiring stitches. When relatives told this story, they laughed. Art, around seventy when he last spoke of this with me, grinned with lips and teeth, but his eyes winced at my questions: "Where did this happen?" "Did he say 'sorry'?" I felt shame. Still do.

As a boy, when Papa visited cousins he made the girls play "funeral" with their dolls, complete with barnyard burials. If they did not cry, he pinched them until they demonstrated proper grief.

He focused on weaker people with vise-grip headlocks, ear twisting, knuckles grinding into skulls. Passing me as I sat at the kitchen table eating a snack, he often asked whether I would like a *klap voor de kop* ("smack in the head") or servings of *overslag* ("being hit again"), his idea of a joke.

As early as I can remember he wrestled with me too. This went on until I was an adolescent. Unlike my namesake cousin Art, I never needed stitches, but he, a classic bully, stopped when I grew muscles enough to compete, disappointing me because I wanted to match, if not best, him just once.

＞＜

And yet, I admired my dad, as small boys—even, perhaps especially, fearful little boys—invariably do.

I must have been a little unsure of his skills at times though, even worried. His first trade was as a house painter. I'd seen the potential hazards on TV cartoons and each time he left for work, I cautioned, "Don't paint yourself into a corner!"

I bemoaned his absences. When I was a preschooler, he was frequently away Mondays to Fridays at long-distance jobs. I told Robby, "I only have a Papa on weekends."

I boasted too.

Robby and I argued in his backyard sandbox one day. He said that his father was the strongest man in the world. I claimed that my dad had not only painted all the neighborhood's houses but also all white lines down the middle of all roads. I liked leaning against the car window watching those marks blur by, whenever our family rode anywhere.

＞＜

I wished my father would play with me. Instead, at home, he smoked, sipped Old Vienna or Canada Club, watched wrestling on TV, read the newspaper, snarled at newscasters.

As a small lad, the way to get close to my often-absent father was through his work, sometimes tagging along to work sites. I'd borrow a brush and slap water here and there, pretending to paint.

At least once I wandered dangerously from home, inadvertently drawn to water.

Three years old, I took my tricycle on a jaunt. My mother was distracted, perhaps with the laundry, perhaps with my baby sister. I found it hard to gain traction on gravel, but my pudgy legs pushed hard on the pedals and I conquered the twenty-five-yard driveway. Reaching the busy street, I turned right. Two-lane Martindale Road plummeted a hundred feet, ending near a roiling canal. Not able to keep my feet on the whirling pedals, I careened and wobbled, but stayed astride, cold spring air forcing my watering eyes shut and biting at my ears, stinging my cheeks. I eventually coasted to a halt within yards of the turbulent water, the kind of hazard that keeps parents awake at night. I enjoyed the view.

Perhaps the police officer happened to be passing, maybe someone phoned in a report. My mother cannot remember. My trike now in the trunk, I sat on the front seat, the trip back up as thrilling as my descent— certainly more enjoyable than cruiser rides decades later as an apprehended protester, sitting in the rear, unable to open doors or roll down windows, hands cuffed behind me.

The cop scolded my startled mother, telling her to do better at watching me. She, pondering how close I came to dangerous waters, was uninterested in my adventurous account. She had never known I was in peril.

SEVEN

So much hostility, so much outrage, spewed in so many different directions. I hardly know what to make of it.

I wonder now whether my father was depressed, perhaps chronically. Did he wish for a different life? He regularly said, "I wish I was a beautiful woman." We laughed, unsure what to make of this. Was this a reference to his father beating him for not being a girl?

Were there unfulfilled creative sides, ones he never permitted himself to pursue? He sang in a resonant tenor at church; when I stood nearby I could hold tunes. Driving, he whistled with more vibrato than Roger Whittaker, a folk singer heard often on the radio. While a young man he drummed in a jazz band, until they started getting Sunday night gigs. As a Calvinist obliged to honor the Sabbath, he withdrew. When I began to write as a teen, my mother told me that during his first days in Canada he freelanced for Dutch periodicals, reporting on the immigrant experience. But I never knew him to spend much time on artistic outlets. He only sang in church, whistled in the car, drummed his pencil on his plate and against his glass at the dinner table. And his writing had long since disappeared. That he established an eventually successful business and invented a Canadian-style greenhouse proved his creativity and inventiveness, but I wonder whether it was enough. All his life he brimmed with frustration and hostility.

When Pa complained about red tape or laws that made no sense to him, he said, "The government," pausing for effect, then always adding, "in its infinite wisdom."

When seeing a face he disliked on TV, maybe a politician or an aristocrat, he called the man a *groote lul*, "big prick." He dismissed outspoken women as "dingbats," especially Maureen McTeer, the wife of short-term Prime Minister Joe Clark, loathing her for retaining her birth name when getting married. He disliked the appearance of many women on TV, comparing their faces to *bloote konten*, "bare bums." He loathed TV pundits and public intellectuals, especially those inclined to the left, regarding them as dupes of potential communist influence, dismissing them as "semi-intellectuals," a label he eventually applied to me.

Every night after supper and then before bed, he turned on the news. When protesters were interviewed or union members picketed or public complaints aired, he spat, "bellyachers," always dismissing introspection and retrospection.

≡≡

My father also had strong food preferences. I do not remember my sister fussing about food, or my mother for that matter. That was a male prerogative.

He never touched chicken. Soldiers sent by ship from the Netherlands to Indonesia after the Second World War ate lots of canned poultry. After two years of that he refused to put another morsel of chicken in his mouth ever again.

His hunger displayed surprising susceptibility to suggestion. A slightly off-color turn to the conversation—referring to bathroom matters or flu effects—immediately displaced desire to eat. His wartime comrades found out about that, and prior to meals they began extended discussions about bodily functions, happy to watch the color drain from his visage as he grimaced and his appetite disappeared. This continued for days until finally my father stormed up to the long table set for a couple dozen men and overturned the whole thing, flipping food, drink, dishes, and cutlery through the air and into the tropical dirt: "If I can't eat, then neither can any of you." He was demoted from corporal to private as a result, but his comrades made sure he never missed another meal.

His touchiness meant censorship at our table. When I was twelve, one of his employees ate lunch with us, something that happened often as the business workshop was behind our house. Omelettes lay on our plates, ready for consumption. "Just think where these eggs came from," said Bill, "squeezed out of the back end of a hen and covered in brown slime." Pa threw down his knife and fork and sped away, his food untouched.

In late summer our rural world was awash in tomatoes. My mother could not can or preserve them all and frantically sought to deal with the overabundance. She fried them with onions and eggs, serving the ensuing mess with toast. Dutch people call this *smurrie* (rhyming with "hurry," meaning "sludge" or "gunk"). My father loathed that term; it made him queasy; he did not permit us to pronounce it in his presence, and we had to warn company. No more tossed tables though.

My mother honored his preferences. He hated the idea of pig meat. When she served *pork* chops, he asked whether these "pork chops came from a pig or from a cow." She always answered "cow" and still remains unsure whether he believed in beef-pork or whether polite deceit contented him. Denial and avoidance had its uses.

≡

At times he seemed deliberately comical, but it was hard to be sure. He jutted his full set of dentures from his mouth, crinkled and crossed his eyes, and slid his spectacles down his nose. Was he clowning or mocking an ethnic group?

He never pronounced "throw" correctly, always "strow," no matter how often we objected. Obstinate or provocative?

When he wielded his pencil to stir cream into coffee or milk into tea—never using a spoon—was he trying to prove lack of sophistication or just being absent-minded?

When he cracked hard-boiled eggs on his head, was this supposed to amuse us or was he hoping that my little sister Margaret and I would try—and fail? We often hit ourselves with the pointed end rather than the bluntly rounded end. He chuckled when we fell for the trick.

≡

My father Pleun was reckless about many things. In hotels and convention centers, it amused him to pull fire alarms and then stand off to the side, waiting and watching as clanging ensued. When sirens neared, he smirked, never owning up to authorities.

Startled friends would ask: "What are you doing?"

"I like the fuss," he'd explain.

They'd shake their heads: "But isn't that illegal?"

"So what? They waste my taxes."

Whenever I was with him in public buildings, I saw him pause beside alarms, weighing and considering whether to do this one more time. He would look at me and grin.

———

A small-statured man, he always wanted to prove himself. Barely five feet six, he was preoccupied with size. He forbade my mother from wearing high heels at their wedding because she might then appear the taller one.

Over dinner at age ten, I mentioned stopping at the corner store to persuade its new owner to subscribe to *TV Guide* as part of my route. My father said of the proprietor's wife: "I don't like her. Short women are bossy and mean," a comment I wish I had never heard, something I wish to forget. The claim always seemed absurd—superstitious at best, malicious at worst. One more ugly notion lodged in my memory.

Yet being small benefited him. During the War, forged identity papers labeled him as under his actual age of thirteen. That saved him from Nazi conscription for slave labor.

In elementary school, he played and sang the role of Rumpelstiltskin, *Repelsteeltje*, the bizarrely bitter, gnomic alchemist who turned straw to gold. Later Pa was fascinated by Zacchaeus, the short Bible character frustrated at being stuck in a crowd and unable to see Jesus, the famous preacher. The exploiting tax collector Zacchaeus was also entrepreneurially adept, like *Repelsteeltje*, like my father, spinning wealth from raw opportunities. This is the only Bible text he ever mentioned. He disliked others quoting Scripture, but often sang a Dutch ditty:

> *Zacheus was een kleine man*
> *Dat weet je wel misschien*
> *Hij clom vlug in een hoge boom*
> *Want hij wouw Jezus sien*
> Zacchaeus was a little man
> Maybe you know that
> He quickly climbed a high tree
> Because he wanted to see Jesus.

Often he changed the lyrics to say he wanted to see Roelie, my mom.

One of the few times he spoke of his home life, this only son, this only surviving child, told me, "Well, you could say I was not my father's favorite. My parents had awful arguments. Yelling and insulting. In the middle of one fight, my father pointed at me: 'Son, your mother and I are going to break up. Which parent do you want to live with? Her or me? Choose.'

"I don't know how old I was when this happened. Between four and ten. I started crying. I couldn't make up my mind. Choose? I couldn't decide."

I believed him, but seldom saw my father cry, even though our own family had sorrows aplenty, including my sister's death at the age of seventeen.

As his body lay in the funeral home, one of his friends told me about driving past a park near Lake Ontario a few weeks earlier and seeing my father at a picnic table in the cold spring air. My father—never much for the outdoors, let alone lingering in a park—sat cradling his head in his hands. I was in my mid-thirties and could only guess at his thoughts. Anticipating death, I imagined. He seldom told anyone much about himself or his feelings.

I picture him hunkered beneath tall trees at that table and wish I could have comforted him, perhaps alleviated his life-permeating anger, just as I often wish he had comforted me.

My father regularly boasted that on the first day of kindergarten teachers expelled him for the entire year. During recess, he broke his classroom's toy shovels against a fence, his bad temper already manifest. He never explained what provoked him. Perhaps it was as unconscious as my trike wandering, but it feels more ominous.

In his early twenties he became engaged to a young woman in the Netherlands. The date was set and they began receiving wedding gifts. Then he got into such a row with his future father-in-law that the engagement was aborted, the wedding cancelled, and most gifts returned. A few years later, his former fiancée married my father's half-uncle and became my dad's aunt. In the following decades, my father and his formerly intended kept tensely silent about each other and what exactly happened.

His reputation for rage endured.

As a teenager, I spent school holidays in his workshop, running a Rube Goldberg device—wheels, fan belts, jagged saw blade—intended to cut lengths of galvanized pipe or extruded aluminum. That machine frequently broke down. One day, frustrated by the latest problems, my father took a pipe wrench and hammered at the contraption with Thor-like fury. I looked on, ten feet away, saying nothing, wanting to disappear, become invisible, hoping to stay safe, flinching as iron clanged over and over against iron. We needed that apparatus though, so he called a handyman to repair it. When Mr. Bax, a Dutchman who lived nearby, arrived and saw machine pieces mounded on the cement floor, he quietly asked a question for which he expected no answer: "Your dad lose his temper again?"

≡

When he and my mother were courting, she once broke off their dating as he was still obsessed with his ex-fiancée. During that hiatus my mom went to a church picnic with another young man. Pleun showed up and insisted she ride home with him. She declined, pointing out that she had come with someone else. Cursing, he kicked out pegs of the tent that had been set up to shelter the food and drinks.

My mother still expresses mystification at his rages. She told me recently: "He acted so crazy at times. I couldn't understand. I didn't know what to do, where it came from. I read an article about war vets last week. I am starting to suspect he maybe had PTSD." And then I remember reading: "Entering the world of trauma is like looking into a fractured looking glass."[*]

≡

If so, from where did it come?

Like many lads, he was endangered during the Nazi Occupation. The Germans erected street corner roadblocks and raided houses door-to-door, searching for eligible males (fourteen years and older) to conscript for slave labor. In the final year of the war Pa hid with a cousin in the attic while Nazi

* Francine Shapiro and Margot Silk Forest, *EMDR: Eye Movement Desensitization and Reprocessing* (New York: Basic Books, 1997), 49.

officers were billeted in the house. The boys were warned to keep quiet and not to clamber out onto the roof to pee into the gutter, especially at night.

After the Second World War, Pa volunteered for the Dutch army; he wanted to be a man, perhaps even a paratrooper.*

Recruiters refused my father's application because of his thick glasses and flat feet. He and his father visited an officer that the family knew, and Pleun tearfully appealed the appraisal. Paperwork was rewritten. More falsified records. He entered the infantry and headed overseas, in time getting promoted. After the table flipping demotion, he eventually received another promotion but was demoted again—this time for striking an officer who insulted my father's platoon.

The harrowing years of malaria and tropical fighting marked my father for the rest of his life. He often awoke yelling and drenched in sweat.

⇒⇐

And then there was his father. My father said little about his dear dad, a dark aspect of his life much like his war exploits. Actually, darker and deeper. He shared some Indonesian stories—how he started to smoke there because of stress; how whizzing bullets snapped off nearby bamboo during his first firefight; how he shot a twelve-foot python that had escaped from a zoo. He never answered my questions about whether he killed anyone, never spoke of hearing others scream or watching comrades die. Yet he showed more openness about reporting selected aspects of that horrific war than about his father. But once, when I was thirty-two, he said something about his own father that I also feel about him: "One reason I'm sorry that he's been gone such a long time is because I'd like to sit down and have a good talk with him."

---

* *Indonesian War for Independence*: When Japan abandoned its occupation of Indonesia, many Indonesians wanted independence, but the Dutch waged a military campaign to reclaim the colony. Shortly after World War II, the media and public war-weary, this colonial action did not get much press. Netherlanders, humiliated for years by Nazis, turned their resentment on others. In countries, as in families, the abused easily become the abusers. Decades later, reports of atrocities emerged: 100,000 Indonesians killed and 5,000 Dutch casualties.

EIGHT

My father fuelled himself, as his Glazen Stad father and uncles did, with anger, alcohol, and ambition. He resented statutory holidays and the annual weeklong vacation that my mother insisted he take. Boers men lived hard and died young. My father lived to sixty-three. His father died a few days before turning sixty. Assuming they would not get old, they raced to accomplish and accumulate before heart attacks or cancer inevitably triumphed.

My father loathed memories of being a poor immigrant. In his last years he daily crammed his wallet with a couple thousand dollars to exorcise that shame. He steadily acquired savings and investments, never planning to retire. "I don't want your mother to worry about money," he told me a few months before he died. He could not take anything with him but wanted to leave a lot behind.

In his early thirties, Pa began working for a large greenhouse building company in Canada. Dissatisfied as an employee—he wanted to give the orders and earn more—he went into business for himself, first repairing and building greenhouses and eventually inventing and manufacturing his own designs for sturdy structures that withstood deep snowfall. He likened them to ready-to-assemble Erector Sets.

He sheathed walls and roofs with glass, an expertise called "glazing," something I hoped to learn someday. In subzero Fahrenheit temperatures, glazing nails would freeze to his skin. He wore sturdy fingerless woollen mitts that my mother had knit. He cut, fit, and placed panes between puttied bars, work that was prone to mishaps. The glass often slipped and slid, or cracked unexpectedly, drawing blood. White scars crisscrossed his fingers, hands, and arms.

By the time he died, his business had glassed over hundreds of square miles of land. Those greenhouses lengthened growing seasons by capturing sunlight all year, helping vegetables thrive and flowers flourish—cucumbers, peppers, tomatoes, lettuce; mums, poinsettias, carnations, cacti.

He never discussed God and often disparaged my "fanatic" interest in theology. He felt frustrated with my ascetic lifestyle and raged against my university philosophy studies. But he did teach me his greenhouse *ethics*. "I feel better," he told me, "when farmers raise food, something people need. Flowers are a luxury." Yet I believe in beauty and blooms, especially when I see how happy they make my wife, my mother, hosts we visit, sick parishioners. Even my father himself took comfort in tulips in the days before he died.

His designs, small Glazen Stads in themselves, migrated from Ontario to Nova Scotia and British Columbia, Florida and California, and overseas to mainland China, Saudi Arabia, Libya.

His proudest achievement was exporting his unique model to the Netherlands, land of his birth and world's greenhouse capital, even into the Glazen Stad. This eighth-grade-educated, self-made immigrant liked impressing "old country" relatives. I too am impressed—to an extent.

My father never studied engineering. He attended school until age fourteen and then learned the house-painting trade. What he knew about greenhouses he discovered through trial and error. He never went to business school but built a company that ultimately thrived.

His enterprising helped grow flowers and plants, employed dozens of men, and fed and clothed my mother, sister, and me. Our family lived simply but seldom lacked necessities, even in the leanest years. Glazed acres paid for our clothes, food, and medicine; they employed me in summers and ensured that university entailed no debt for me or my children; and they defrayed mortgages, mine and theirs. He died three decades ago, but my mother still never needs to worry. I am grateful for that fiscal legacy, for his achievements—to an extent.

Yet I resented his long work hours—six days a week, with him often disappearing to his office or workshop in the evenings—and his frequent absences. Now in my sixties, I lament that I only had a Papa until my mid-thirties. I wish that we had more time.

As far as I can remember, my hand held his glass-scarred hand only once, and that during his last moments.

My hands and heart have scars; my father's had more. He laid glass on roofs and in walls, etching surfaces with diamond-tipped glass cutters and then snapping the panes (also called "lights") along the markings. When frustrated, Pa Frisbeed fragments across construction sites, his employees running for cover from the sharp shrapnel. Even without rage, glass was dangerous, threatening skin and muscles, blood vessels, even limbs.

The last time I visited my father's cousin Art—he was seventy-one, had been hospitalized for two months, and unbeknownst to us would die two days later—I asked him about working for my father during high school summer vacations. "I was lucky. I fell through glass a couple times but wasn't really hurt," he told me. Not all were as fortunate.

One greenhouse farmer, Mr. Van Putten, toppled from a scaffold through a roof, carving up his left arm. It never again worked properly. I watched him months later, unable to lift the door of the garage where my father stored and sold glass. Cradling a self-rolled cigarette in his right hand, its smoke curling upward, he sounded matter-of-fact: "It could have been worse. I might have lost the arm. Maybe died." His fatalism felt familiar.*

Such stoicism impressed me, perhaps I envied it. Perhaps I still do, as I ponder my childhood. That too could have been worse.

---

* *Dutch fatalism*: Dutch Calvinists struck me as fatalistic. Many events, I was told, were beyond our control. God precisely numbered our days and we must not tamper with that. "In thy book were written, every one of them, the days that were formed for me" (Ps. 139:16). "And which of you by being anxious can add one cubit to his span of life?" (Matt. 6:27). "Lord, let me know my end, and what is the measure of my days" (Ps. 39:4).

Calvin and Augustine understood predestination to be about salvation or damnation but I heard adults connect predestination to the precisely calibrated length of life. We could not extend our lives and must not indulge in risky behavior—stunts, extreme sports—that tempted God. There were paradoxes. How could we shorten our lives if our days were numbered? Why engage in medical procedures to extend lives if days were numbered? On the other hand, there was also a strange consolation for some. When someone died—even tragically—their time had come. When my sister perished at age seventeen, our pastor—who had lost a young daughter himself—counseled: "It's best not to think about these things."

Over the years, Pa and I drove all over southern Ontario. His intensely blue eyes behind the thick lenses of his glasses, his dark brown hair slicked back over his head. From the passenger seat I studied his silhouette and the receding chin that made him self-conscious, the one he tried to cover whenever he could by propping a hand under his head.

I sat beside him in his pickup as we drove up and down the Niagara Escarpment, a five-hundred-mile limestone ridge stretching from Niagara Falls to Tobermory. We rode beside the Great Lakes Erie and Ontario, through Holland Marsh's drained acres of black dirt, on bridges across the placid Trent River. He commented on every greenhouse we passed.

"I built that."

"There's one by Lord and Burnham, my old bosses; they use too much steel and iron."

"I did that job for an elder in our church. The hypocrite still hasn't paid, after five years."

"There's Tim's place; supposedly my friend, he keeps asking for cheaper prices but never buys anything from me."

I still do double takes when I pass greenhouses. Every hothouse tells a story. Glazen Stad descendants didn't live in glass houses, but our lives were shaped by them.

NINE

When God first spoke to me, I heard an assignment.

Our functional, red brick, two-story church squatted on Scott Street in St. Catharines, dwarfing the neighborhood's gray stucco 1940s-era bungalows. Tall enough to accommodate a pipe organ and balcony, the high nave conveyed capaciousness even when a couple hundred congregants crowded inside. Varnished, unforgiving pews filled the space, stern seats that left us squirming but solemn. Their oak bore few scratches or graffiti.

The cover of our hymnbook, the *Psalter Hymnal*, featured gold lettering and the outline of an elaborate Gothic church window, its pointed arch hinting at stained glass. But our tall opaque windows, mostly filmy white, presented nothing; they prevented distractions. Lower panes had colors, green, red, and yellow, but no designs, symbols, or Bible stories. No images—graven or glass or otherwise—for us.

Atop a dozen steps, a massive pulpit dominated our sacred austerity, the preacher always preaching and praying well over our heads. Below it a cumbersome table bore the words "Do This in Remembrance of Me"; and we remembered, every three months or so.*

Near the communion table sat a large oak chest with "God Loves a Cheerful Giver" carved into its wood, awaiting our weekly offerings, col-

---

* *Restricted communion*: Only adult members of our congregation were allowed to take the Lord's Supper. Once a teen—usually around eighteen—did profession of faith (comparable to confirmation in other traditions) they were regarded as full members, eligible to vote at meetings and receive communion. Christian Reformed guests on a Lord's Supper Sunday had to meet with the elders before the service and present their credentials before getting approved to take part. Visitors from other denominations need not apply.

lected in red velvet bags with varnished wooden handles, passed from the aisles by deacons.

Hearing about Solomon or Jesus at the temple, Moses or David's tabernacle, or any Bible sanctuary (even the pagan shrine Samson demolished), I always pictured our tall off-white walls and elongated brass light fixtures dangling above. Little Samuel surely heard God's voice in such a room, asleep on the floor next to the offering chest, in front of the deacons.

The organ accompanied us, pipes rumbling above like God's voice from on high, outthundering hearty unison singing. Before I could decipher lyrics I moved my lips and hummed, pretending to mouth words, wanting to participate. Several years later, when I could read, I sang so loudly that nearby children looked askance. I liked being noticed by others, liked proving my devotion.

Children, all of us scrubbed and bathed the night before, did not run around, did not bring toys or coloring books. We went to the bathroom beforehand and if the need struck during the service, we pressed legs and clenched buttocks, squirming. If we had to speak, we whispered. I remember our shock, commented on for years, when a young father with a Trudeaumania* haircut toted his little boy from church mid-service, the tiny tantrum thrower yelling, "You idiot!" All of us unsettled not just by the outburst but by poor parenting. They obviously spoiled him.

We had little liturgical drama. A few minutes before worship began, a dozen deacons, men in suits, entered the northeastern doors and moved to designated rows in the eastern transept. Then elders, more men, filed through northwestern doors, mirroring diaconal counterparts, into the western transept. The minister emerged in black Geneva gown and shook hands with the chairman of the elders. Then the *Dominee* (meaning "minister" and pronounced "dough-meh-nay") mounted the stairway. A few years later Reverend Kuntz innovated. He gave up the gown, preferring a plain suit, and ran up those steps, bouncing into position with a jolly grin. He loved his job, we figured. My parents and I approved of his informality and enthusiasm.

Worship included long, solemn prayers and the central feature was a sermon focusing on a Bible verse or phrase within a verse. The preaching

---

* Fans of Prime Minister Pierre Elliott Trudeau often paid tribute to the charismatic national leader by imitating his Caesar-style hair, combing it forward into straight bangs that distracted from receding hairlines.

went on for twenty-five minutes or more. The Scriptures often told us to come back that afternoon for the second service, not to shop or go to movies or swim on Sundays, and to be sure to support Christian schools during the week.

I found it hard to sit through all this, especially as we arrived half an hour early for preferred seats off to the side. Time accumulated. I had to be quiet and had nothing to do. No books or toys or entertainment were permitted. No snacks except for three King's peppermints that my mother doled out near the start of the service. Margaret quickly crunched hers, but I let each one dissolve in my mouth, savoring the white brightness, only biting when it thinned to the thickness of paper. I timed my consumption to have one for the final benediction. Every three months, I set one aside until adults ate the body of Christ, precisely measured and diced cubes of bread. I wanted to do this in remembrance too.

I did not understand much during my first years in church. Yet one service riveted me when I was four. Unusually, we had a guest speaker. Normally only our pastor spoke. On rare occasions when he could not, grave illness perhaps, an elder read one of the minister's prepared sermons. This day's guest, however, was "our" missionary in Nigeria. He had grown up in our church and his fruit farmer parents looked on proudly, a few pews away from us.

I enjoyed the slides—our church seldom had visuals—and studied surprising images of people in brightly colored clothing. I had never encountered a Black person. Thatched roofs looked strange, like something from Bible stories. Touched that we helped faraway people, I wanted to donate dimes and pennies from the Empire State Building bank that sat on my dresser back at home, the one beside the stuffed baby alligator that Opa and Oma brought me after their Florida vacation.

I sensed then that God had something in mind for me, some work. I sat with blond hair slicked, starched white collar constricting my neck, woolen pants pricking my legs, feet dangling between pew and parquet. God encountered me then and there.

We were sitting near the deacons and I looked up at the slight missionary, with his black horn-rims and shy voice, and felt overcome, knowing God wanted my attention. Perhaps I heard a voice, like the one that beckoned Samuel in a space like ours, not far from our pew. An inner certainty washed through me. On that day, I felt a "call," though the missionary nei-

49

ther invited nor encouraged such a response, though I never heard anyone speak in church of a call, though none of my relatives were ministers, missionaries, or even Christian schoolteachers.

I hardly knew what to make of this, my first mystical experience. I only knew that God had something for me to do.

Our family had no sense of talking to, let alone hearing from, God. Ours was a formal relationship with the deity. My parents disparaged pious people and laughed about relatives who sang, "I Will Make You Fishers of Men" while riding in their car. We respected clergy but knew them to be different. We did not sit in the front row. We did not befriend ministers. Down-to-earth people exerting our bodies, we did real work.

My aunt, uncle, and cousins came to our house after church for Dutch pastries, called *gebakkjes*—featuring sweetness and whipped cream, berries and chocolate and mocha. On the floor at the varnished pine coffee table, eyeing McIntoshes piled in the multi-colored glass fruit bowl, sipping iced orange Freshie, I announced: "At church, God told me I'm supposed to work for him, maybe like that missionary."

Adults said nothing.

A cousin laughed, from unease not mockery, I think.

Grown-ups asked no questions, offered no affirmations, but spoke of our "blessings."

"Did you see how poor those Nigerians are?"

"Imagine living in a mud hut with no running water."

No one else ever mentioned my call. I pondered it though and wondered about the adults' silence, never forgetting my encounter with God in church that day.

TEN

When I was five, shortly before beginning kindergarten, we moved north-east, diagonally from the city's southwest corner, to Port Weller East, an isolated area on the other side of the Welland Canal, a bridge the only connection to the rest of the city. We moved for my father's business. His greenhouse repairing and building required workshop space, not to mention room for storing stacks of wood, galvanized pipes, angle iron, cans of paint and pails of putty, boxes of nails, screws, washers, and, of course, *kists* and *kists* of glass.

The real estate agent, misleading my parents, claimed that the $7,700 property was zoned for business. They committed to a mortgage they could hardly afford. Dead-end Yonge Street contained half a dozen houses, including our 1920s-era one-and-a-half story home, shabbily sheathed with Insulbrick, a tar-coated sheeting pressed to resemble red bricks and black mortar. Beyond the end of our yard, land dropped to the canal, a couple hundred yards away, and the Seaway Haulage Road ran between us and water that slapped against concrete embankments. Once, when neighbor boys played baseball with me on our grass, my friend batted an Indian rubber ball so hard that it soared high in the air and disappeared, plummeting we were sure into the drink.

Low, short ocean freighters and long, tall Canada Steamship Line lakers passed day and night. We peered through our windows at vessels that appeared to sail along the edge of our property. For the first weeks their loud horns woke us during the night. Gradually, we grew accustomed to the sound and then smiled when overnight guests complained of the noise.

Acquaintances in other parts of St. Catharines looked startled when they heard where we now lived. Our neighborhood, on the wrong side of the ca-

51

nal, had a reputation and not a good one. Low-income families and impoverished seniors crammed year-round into flimsy one- or two-bedroom cottages with no basements, former summer vacation houses that were uninsulated against the biting north winds that blew straight off Lake Ontario.

I got to know the neighborhood better a few years later when I delivered *TV Guide*s on Friday afternoons after school and collected outstanding accounts on Saturday mornings. (This seemed better than working a paper route six days a week.) Many unkempt yards had tall weeds and large patches of mud that were filled with beer, wine, and whiskey bottles. I disliked the squalor. Some homes smelled of deep-fried fat and rancid meat, so I knocked on doors and held my breath. I asked my mother whether I could abandon clients whose houses reeked, but she forbade that. Businesspeople do not refuse customers.

Not all the yards were ugly. My mother transformed ours into a garden of promise.

⊒⊏

The previous owner, elderly immigrant Mr. Olsson, returned to Sweden, his birthplace, and left behind a house filled with furniture, dishes, pots, and pans. Not to mention fumes, soot, dust, canine hair, and dog shit. His large dogs had had free rein in the basement. Their scents never fully dissipated and worsened in damp weather. Persistent mustiness and acrid urine odors scraped our nostrils for seven years. In the basement, I avoided dark squiggling floor stains that never disappeared. I assumed them all to be fecal.

Oma Ganzevoort and my father's aunt, Tante Stien, joined my mother in a Dutch cleaning blitz, scrubbing the house's surfaces. My parents kept much of Olsson's abandoned cutlery, dishes, pots, pans, and furniture. Having lived only in small apartments, they had few possessions. They gave me one of his single beds and a discarded dresser; I used both until graduating from university. They furnished my room with a squeaky antique secretary's desk, where I learned to study and write through grade school and then high school. I still own it.

The neglected half-acre yard was mostly weeds. Skinny teenage cousin Art, ten years older than I, removed his shirt and scythed waist-high weeds.

I wanted to try that, but my mother warned that scythes were hazardous for children.

With his trailer, Opa bounced broken furniture and moldy boxes to the dump. I noticed that a beloved toy, a hobby horse, was missing and clamored about this to my parents. They tried putting me off, but I persisted. Finally, Opa conceded that it may have been included in one of his trips. My father, mother, Opa, and I rode to the landfill and walked the wobbly surface of discards, trying to find where our refuse landed.

Much to everyone's relief—because I was so distraught and such a noisy nuisance—we found it. I don't recall ever playing with it again though.

———

In the yard, Opa pruned two parallel rows of apple and pear trees, three of each. Every year my mother would can pears and make applesauce. Week after week, she mowed the lawn for three-hour stretches. As weeds gradually diminished, a lawn appeared. She tended roses that had gone wild and planted hydrangeas and peonies in front of the house and along the length of the yard. Bees buzzed. I chased garters in the grass and climbed fruit trees and the tall chestnut that towered in front of the house. The yard became, in its own way, a place of beauty.

My parents granted me a dirt mound, six by six feet, in a back corner, overlooking the canal. I could dig all the way to hell or China, whichever came first, but never got deeper than two or three feet. I built castles and roads, planted watermelon and pumpkin seeds, and dug trenches where I enacted battles with plastic soldiers and jeeps and a bridge that would pop in two when I touched a lever at its side, sending vehicles and troops flying.

When we moved in, there was a rusty steel swing set and wooden slide with a surface that was not slideable (so Margaret and I crawled up and ran down instead). In the summers, my parents set up a tall teepee between the pear and apple trees, an outdoor playroom. A couple nights every July, my sister and I overnighted there, rolling up in Dutch woollen blankets, the closest we ever came to camping.

Tall evergreens lined our driveway, fifty-foot sentinels, majestic as the oversized Christmas trees of capitol squares—spruces, two white and a blue. We pointed them out to guests, boasting, "People tell us that those are worth a lot of money."

⇒⇐

I chased rabbits. I'd spot them through windows when I was up early, looking from my bedroom upstairs or downstairs from the living room. Or when I was visiting my parents in bed—only on a Sunday of course, the one day that they slept in, and only for a little while because we always went to church and we always went early.

I would grab shoes and race outside, still in my pajamas. Rabbits would dash off, dodging and weaving down the yard, disappearing into weeds, bouncing into bushes beyond our chain-link fence. I set up a cardboard box, a trap learned from Opie on *The Andy Griffith Show*, propped it with a stick attached to a string, and strategically placed bread slices inside. I waited for a creature to hop underneath so I could yank the stick. None ever neared it.

As I scampered after rabbits my parents would watch from their bedroom. After futile quests I'd return to them and debrief, recounting my woes and climbing into their strangely consoling bed. During sick days, Margaret and I did not stay in our unheated upstairs bedrooms but in that bed, where we could be near Mom as she cooked, laundered, or cleaned. It's also where I would awaken after my father beat me into a blackout.

⇒⇐

Upstairs, the polished hardwood landing proved ideal for setting up plastic bowling pins at one end and then rolling plastic balls at them, watching them fly apart and listening to their hollow clatter. I never did this long, quickly tiring of resetting pins.

In my room Venetian blades rattled in the drafts and hindered the light—but not the sounds of children playing outside long after my bedtime. Puzzle pieces fell through the wide pine floorboards of my walk-in closet and could not be retrieved. In a cupboard there, painted light pink, I stored my Etch A Sketch, random rocks, magic trick resources, *Classics Illustrated* comics, a few foreign coins, and a bag of marbles.

Paneled wood squares along the stairwell wall fascinated me. Surely, as I'd seen in TV shows, they must hide a secret room, a place to be completely alone and totally safe. Ascending or descending, I pressed different combinations of squares, looking for a disguised latch. I knocked, hoping to detect hollowness that would indicate a dark cobwebbed space waiting to be discovered, perhaps even a trove of riches, preferably in a locked chest.

I always longed for protected places and for treasure, searching for adventure even as I yearned for safety.

$$=\!\!=\!\!=$$

Our unfinished cellar with its bare plastered walls had no straight edges or corners, unlike friends' finished basements in enviably new subdivisions. But while the lingering dog poop scents gave me pause, those lower spaces sparked my imagination.

Mom laundered in a room that accommodated laundry tubs and her clothes wringer, with rope lines slung through the room for when outside weather did not cooperate. Next to it the furnace chamber, the length of our house, held more drying lines and at one end a small door opened onto a sump pump closet.

In the front below-ground room my mother shelved canned goods, but she also placed chairs, table and blackboard for Margaret and me. We used that space for games, entertaining other children, playing school, and fantasizing about rocket ships or ocean liners.

When Dutch guests stayed with us my mother loaned them my room and set up an army cot for me in the front basement room.*

As I waited to sleep in that basement room, my mother whisked our kittens—Smokey (the first of a half dozen Smokeys in my life) and Pinky—through the basement door. After thumping down the stairs, disconsolately I thought, they would notice me across the room, then bound over and jump atop me. With rudely intrusive affection they'd scratch my ears with their

---

* *Summer visitors*: Every year we had company from Holland. Aunts, uncles, and cousins came and stayed for one or two weeks, my grandmother every other year for a month and a half. We always took guests to Niagara Falls. On Sunday afternoons, they could attend worship conducted in Dutch at our church. We looked forward to visits. I got to speak Dutch and guests brought treats. My parents liked *paling*, smoked eel, but Margaret and I preferred *droppies*, Dutch licorice. One year my grandmother brought a magazine about the Beatles—she was a fan—and I climbed into the chestnut tree to read it.

tongues. Since they were normally segregated from us overnight, never allowed in bedrooms, this seemed a special treat, for them and me.

≡≡

Natural light saturated our south-facing house. The front hall had so many windows—along with an etched glass door with bevelled panes dividing it from the living room—that it resembled a conservatory. My mother filled it with greenery.

The deep sills of our living room bay window accommodated plants. When prestige-conscious Dutch relatives visited, Tante Pie scolded Oom Rien for standing in front of that window while wearing a vest without its properly accompanying suit jacket, even when no one was outside to see. Seldom did anyone walk or drive the quiet street that dead-ended at a large wooden barrier overlooking the cement-banked canal. Cars that appeared on the street overnight were often abandoned there after joyrides, waiting to be identified by police and then towed. Across from our house sat two vacant properties, expropriated by the St. Lawrence Seaway Commission, the agency that oversaw the canal's operation.

The dead-end meant we could play tag and hockey on pavement without fear of traffic. On Victoria Days neighborhood dads gathered children there and lit fireworks—one of the few times we saw our fathers play, let alone include us in revelry. To a degree, that is; only dads could wield and light matches. But children were allowed to twirl sprinklers and toss cherry bombs; after mothers warned about lost fingers and blinded eyes.

Gritty black chimney soot belched from passing ships, incessantly infiltrating our house, steadily creeping through casement gaps. With our many windows, soot had lots of access. In Dutch houses, though, glass must glint. So my mother, in addition to perpetually vacuuming and wiping dark grit from sills, regularly polished panes.

In the fall, she would climb a ladder in her dress—she always wore dresses, even during yard work, until the day a dozen yellow jackets swarmed up her skirt. She would remove the screens in their heavy wooden frames, carry them down and rinse them in the yard. She washed all windows, inside and out. Then she would retrieve heavy storm windows from the basement and scour them on the lawn before carrying them up ladders and securing them. My father never helped. He was accustomed to ladders at work but did not labor in or around our house, not even occasionally washing dishes. In the spring my mother reversed the process, removing storm windows, cleaning them and the house windows, sweeping and rinsing screens, and remounting them.

That clarity, though, was a hazard to wildlife. Birds regularly thudded against glass. One Sunday, Opa, the roadkill hunter, surprised us with unexpected tenderness. All of us were enjoying refreshments and pastries in the living room after church. We heard a small thump, and he headed outside, bent down beside the garden, and cradled a small feather bundle. Soon, the house sparrow shrugged and fluffed itself before launching from his open palm. Opa explained the resurrection: "Sometimes, they're just stunned and need rest and warmth."

In this house I still tried to connect with my dad, even though he was never much for playing.

One Sunday afternoon, when I was eight or so, we had been to church, and I was determined to change his pattern. He sat at the end of the couch, reading the newspaper with a cup of coffee nearby and the eternally present cigarette, smoke drifting upward. Soon it would be time for a cocktail. He declined my requests to play checkers or Go Fish or *Peste*. Then I had an idea. "What if the living room is a plane and I am the pilot? You could be a passenger. You don't have to do anything."

To this he agreed.

I set up a straight dining room chair for myself near him and imagined an airplane control panel in front of me, pressed buttons and spun a wheel, all invisible, and looked around, commenting quietly on weather conditions and asking him about the headlines he was reading.

My father said nothing.

Every once in a while, I turned: "Are you doing OK, sir? Can I get you anything? Coffee? Something to drink? Do you need anything?"

He did not. He never did.

ELEVEN

I envied doors. *Door* is a Dutch word that means "through."

Patio doors for instance, wide glass panels that slid open for easy access to the outside. What a pleasure. Many acquaintances lived in newer houses, with decks or patios to sit and eat and visit. Our house was older. I wouldn't have patio doors until my mid-thirties.

I liked Dutch doors even more, something I've never had. I knew them from TV. Their top half, a glass window, might swing inward while the bottom half could remain latched. Informal visits and conversations could happen without anyone leaving or entering the house, animals and children stayed in their respective places, and fresh air could move. On *Lassie*, deliveries could be passed through or Timmy's mother could hand out food to passers-by. Dutch doors offer mixed messages, open and closed at the same time. My mother told me that farmers often had them in Holland, the name there being *Boerendeur*, "farmer door." The *boeren* ("farmers") part of the name sounded especially good to me, given our surname. I wished we had a Dutch door too, but unlike with patio doors, I never knew anyone who did, even though most of our acquaintances were Dutch.

I puzzled at how we immigrants were and were not separated from others. Anyone who was not Dutch, our family labeled "Canadians," no matter their ethnicity. The distinctions—and connections—were partial, not entire. They were like the half-hearted separations of Dutch doors, partly porous and partly impermeable, partially open and partially protected. Much as Dutch culture itself. It is known for tolerance and hospitality toward various faiths, but *within* traditions each Dutch Calvinist sect allowed little room for doctrinal digression.

—=—

Back on Martindale Road, our previous home, Dutch people were all around. Neighbors in our two-flat were Heckmans. They were followed by a couple, who happened to be surnamed "Boers" like us but who were not our relatives, even though John Boers also hailed from the Glazen Stad and built greenhouses. Next door, I regularly visited the Boots. Various nationalities lived nearby in Port Weller where we moved—British, Norwegian, Italian—but even there we found ample Dutch households. Three Tuinder families dwelled a block away on Broadway Avenue; they owned a range of greenhouses. When I was eight, the Saus family moved a block from our house to start a garden nursery with greenhouses.*

Two Saus sons, Johnny and Ricky, one and two years younger than I, became my best friends in the neighborhood. One day, we played hide-and-seek, running with bursts of energy through their front yard. Their father called and ordered us to load potted plants into the back of the station wagon. This done, Johnny casually slammed the back hatch. The entire window loudly dissolved and cascaded into tiny fragments onto the gravel. None of us understood what happened, but their father exploded, as fathers sometimes did, yelling and swearing. I slunk quietly home. The next day my mom told me that their dad was in the hospital with a "nervous breakdown."

—=—

At home my parents spoke mostly Dutch.

The last thing Margaret and I said each day was *welterusten* ("rest well"). In the morning we sang out *goede morgen* ("good morning") as we exited bedrooms and descended the stairs into the dining room. To this day, when speaking with my mother on the phone or in person, I never notice whether she opts for Dutch or English. She randomly mixes both.

* *Dutch Canadian greenhouses and nurseries*: "The commercial growing and transportation of flowers . . . is a business dominated by Dutch-Canadians, who control 80 percent of the greenhouse operations in Ontario. About 70 percent of the growers and at least 10 percent of the retail florists in Ontario are of recent Dutch descent." Frans J. Schryer, *The Netherlandic Presence in Ontario: Pillars, Class and Dutch Ethnicity* (Waterloo: Wilfrid Laurier University Press, 1998), 300.

When immigrant neighbors from other countries failed to learn English, my parents said, "What's wrong with those people? We're in Canada." Immigrants should speak English out of the house, they insisted. We just didn't need to prioritize it in our personal life.

There were Dutch periodicals on our coffee table—newspapers, *Nederlandse Courant*, and magazines such as *Spiegel* ("Mirror"). We spoke Dutch with friends and relatives. My father's customers and employees were mostly from the Netherlands. Our congregation was founded by recent immigrants. Everyone shared that ancestry, just like students and teachers and staff at Calvin Memorial Christian School where I would attend from grades one through six.

For years I would not know English terms for gravy, jam, rag, kitchen counter, dustpan, minister. We used Dutch for daily realities. I still have to think hard to recall "rutabaga," even though we ate *koolraapies* weekly in the winter, boiled and salted and covered by white sauce sprinkled with nutmeg.*

Dutch remains my comfort language. I regularly dream in it. In the Netherlands, I think and pray in it. Yet my Dutch is functional, practical, simple—*huis, tuin, keuken* ("house, yard, kitchen"), learned by ear. I do not read or write it. Relatives tell me that I speak a 1950s Glazen Stad dialect, my slang and blunt accent both. I do not have the elevated theological vocabulary or proper grammar for sermons—as I realized when in my late thirties I did a monthlong pulpit exchange with a minister in Holland. Listening to preachers or comedians in the Netherlands, idioms and references do not compute. I have no idea how to recognize eloquent Dutch, what might be lovely or lyrical. For that I have English, and I can be happy an entire day savoring—and murmuring over and over—lyrics or phrases by masterful songwriters, Bruce Cockburn or Fred Eaglesmith,** Mary Gauthier or Lucinda Williams.

---

* *The two most important Dutch words*: No one ever reliably translated *gezellig*, a combination of "convivial" and "cozy," or *leuk*, meaning "fun," "cute," "amazing." Dutch immigrants boast that they cannot be translated. I hear both terms every day when in the Netherlands; obviously people there value togetherness, worthwhile times called *gezellig*; and enjoy fun, being amused, hence an affinity for *leuk*. We hoped that gathering in homes would be *gezellig*; but never did I think that church could be *leuk*.

** Eaglesmith is his stage name; his Frisian birthname is Elgersma. He and I were born the same year and are both children of Dutch immigrants; both of us were raised Christian Reformed in southern Ontario.

But my mother tongue touches a primal level. In my forties, I was waiting in the Detroit airport, and heard over the speakers a random KLM announcement in Dutch detailing the next Amsterdam flight. That gladdened me, happy for mundane details of an upcoming departure, in familiar intonations and pronunciations. Watching Dutch YouTube TV ads I get teary listening to women with permed gray hair who remind me of Omas and elderly Tantes. I hope someone will speak Dutch to me when I am dying, just as I did for my father during his last hours.

Culinary preferences were Dutch, nutmeg on green beans and Brussels sprouts, and chocolate layered on bread. We were leery of other cuisines. Corn on the cob was dismissed as *kippenvoer*, "chicken feed," but Margaret tried it and then my mother, and both recommended it. I was fourteen and unexpectedly found myself agreeing.

A Dutch deli man came to our driveway with Gouda cheese, *cervelat* (sausage), *gerookte paling* (smoked eel) in the back of his station wagon. A Dutch butcher made the rounds in his panel truck with horse meat, slaughtered rabbit, and *tartaar* (spiced hamburger, served raw).

If our house needed repairs, we hired Dutch workers, preferably Christian Reformed. The plumber and electrician were brothers who belonged to our church. For gas and auto repairs we went to the corner of Scott Street and Vine to patronize a Shell station—Shell a Dutch corporation—because its local franchise owner was Dutch, another church member. As we pulled up at the pumps, often spotting others from our congregation, our common ethnicity felt like a shared secret.

A block from the service station, we deposited money in the Dutch credit union. I opened my first bank account there. Next door, we went to the Dutch *winkel*, store, for baked goods, imported or locally prepared, and dry goods (washcloths, handkerchiefs, tea towels, brushes, aprons, underwear—no Canadian products compared). In the same building, we could buy radios and stereos from a Dutchman, who specialized in Philips, another Dutch corporation. I would go to him when I turned thirteen and wanted a tape recorder.

≡≡

In spite of all this, my parents gave me a British name.

On my father's side, custom dictated that the first son—preferably the oldest child—should be named after the paternal grandfather. Great-

61

grandfather Pleun was a stickler. When sons obeyed, calling their eldest "Pleun," compliance earned a baby carriage. Couples who disobeyed received nothing.

Great-grandfather Pleun named three firsts after *his* father. His oldest, my grandfather, was christened "Arie." After great-grandfather's wife died, he married again. Their first-born was a son and also called "Arie." He lived a day. The second-born arrived a year later, another son, and thus another "Arie." Aries go back almost three centuries in our family tree.

As Dutch as they were, my parents altered the alternation, Anglicizing "Arie" into "Arthur." Nowadays ethnic names are common, but in the 1950s cultural conformity was a strong motivator, even for stubborn Dutch immigrants. I liked the royal association, especially after watching Disney's *The Sword in the Stone* in a darkened cinema on St. Paul Street in St. Catharines, peering over the seat and around the head and shoulders in front of me. The film ends on a note of triumph. It would be a long time before I learned that happy endings and heroism often do not endure. King Arthur's certainly didn't.

⊃⊂

But my parents bestowed a name my father could not pronounce.

The Dutch do not have the English "th" sound and enunciate it either "s" or "d" or "t." All my life, Papa called me "Utter" (rhyming with "mutter"). When he died, I saw in his planner that he spelled my name "Artur" and my sister's "Margareth."

In kindergarten, starting school shortly after our move to Port Weller, my teacher, grandmotherly Mrs. Dowling, with gray permed curls and catseye spectacles, tried teaching me how to say my name. When I did not catch on she poked fingers in my mouth to show me where to place my tongue.

TWELVE

On the rare occasions that I'm now invited to preach at a Christian Reformed church—I left that denomination when I was a teen—I request "By the Sea of Crystal." We regularly sang that at Maranatha Christian Reformed, a hymn derived from the book of Revelation.

> "By the sea of crystal, Saints in glory stand,
> Myriads in number, Drawn from every land.
> Robed in white apparel, Washed in Jesus' blood,
> They now reign in heaven, With the Lamb of God."

That image made sense. A popular swimming destination was *Crystal* Beach on Lake Erie. It was an hour-long drive, and we went once a summer. We always returned gritty and badly sunburned, barely able to move enough to play board games, let alone romp outside. For a week following each of these outings, layers of skin would peel from shoulders and backs, and menthol and eucalyptus fragrances would waft from our bodies. We'd slather on Noxzema, hoping the cool greasy lotion would provide relief from sharp pain.

As for the crystal sea, I seldom saw my father cry, but he teared up when we sang that at church. In his imagination he saw beside that glassy water a choir that included his late father, my mother's deceased mother, and, some years later, his daughter who died from complications connected to leukemia.

In our Dutch Calvinist imagination, the hymn was especially apt as water and glass are seldom far apart.

While the Glazen Stad is covered by greenhouse glass, the Netherlands is water saturated. Hence the iconic windmills and engineering ingenuity that drained the country, much of which is below sea level. Dutch people have been known to boast: "God created the earth, but we created Holland."

Sometimes it is hard to know where the water ends and land begins. Like glass itself, Holland is not exactly solid and not exactly liquid. Glass is formed from liquid. Particles, such as sand, are melted in high temperatures and then the fluid is cooled.

Some scientists believe that glass remains a slow-moving liquid, like ice or glaciers.

"Glass is strange. Chemists find it defies their classifications. It is neither a true solid nor a true liquid and is often described as a 'fourth state of matter.'"* In junior high, interested in history, I visited 1800s-era buildings around our small town of St. Davids. I noticed the inconsistent thickness of antique windows. My mother told me that this is because glass, a slow-moving liquid, gradually flows downward, windows steadily melted and glass swelled and accumulated at the bottom. In front of them, I liked to bend my knees and then stand straight, watching scenery outside, trees and buildings, distort and shape-shift, as in a funhouse mirror.

Water and glass are often compared and connected. Sand that rings lakes, oceans, and seas can be a central ingredient for manufacturing glass. A calm prospect over water is "glassy." When a river or lake is transparent, we call it "clear as glass." The edge of heavy panes that my dad wielded were aqua, blue-green, colours of water. Ice on puddles or ponds often appears as a glassed-over surface.

Water, as well as being essential to life, can be dangerous and terrifying. On three occasions, spills while kayaking or canoeing, one in subzero temperatures, could easily have ended with my drowning. A couple of years ago the river in front of our cottage flooded. Water rose over six feet and overran our dead-end road. Like my neighbors, I was stuck on my property for several weeks while emergency helicopters hovered overhead. Canadian military came to bring pharmaceuticals and deliver people to chemother-

* Alan Macfarlane and Gerry Martin, *Glass: A World History* (Chicago: University of Chicago Press, 2002), 3.

apy. United Nations volunteers canvassed house to house to make sure everyone was safe. I had seen floods on the news, but now I experienced one firsthand and marvelled as docks, lawn furniture, oil drums, and over-turned kayaks floated by.

One flood in particular informed my early imagination.

≡≡≡

There were not many options on Sunday afternoons after church. We were not allowed to do homework; that had to be completed by Saturday. Even workaholic men like my father were not permitted to labor.

There was, however, a lot of visiting. Sometimes an invitation was spontaneously extended in the church parking lot during post-worship small talk. Sometimes, especially when folks came from a distance, visiting was arranged well ahead of time. Other times my father or mother proposed a drive after lunch and we wandered roads and highways for an hour or two until one or the other commented, "So-and-so lives near here. I wonder if they're home." Then we'd stop by to check.

Those family, friends, and church members were Dutch, mostly from the Glazen Stad. Adults drank coffee and kids neon-hued orange- or grape-flavored Freshie, a Canadian knock-off of Kool-Aid. Cookies or pastries, either homemade or purchased from Voortmans, a Dutch Canadian company, came on small saucers. Men filled rooms with smoke. If the visit went long enough, shelled peanuts, sour pickled onions, or salty potato chips appeared in tiny bowls, along with whiskey, rum, vermouth, and gin for adults. Children nibbled and then wandered away to find board games or headed outside for hide-and-seek.

I had a reliable strategy if there were no children. Adult conversation did not interest me. Their jokes made no sense although I pretended to laugh. When the TV was off, and if for some reason I had no book (or had finished it in the car), I knew something important about Dutch living rooms. It wasn't just that most had *strookjes*, lace strip curtains, along the top of picture windows, or that thick woollen rugs draped coffee tables, or that one could usually spot wooden shoe ornaments or Delft Blue porcelain or, most intriguingly, a cuckoo clock.

What I knew was that I could almost always find a copy of *De Ramp*, "The Disaster," in a bookcase or on a wall shelf. In 1953, eight years after the end of the Nazi Occupation, the economy still recovering from war, the nation reeled from yet another catastrophe. A high spring tide combined with a severe windstorm, raising sea levels as much as eighteen feet, flooding a fifth of the Netherlands, mostly in the southwest. Eight years before, retreating German soldiers vindictively breached dikes, flooding farms with North Sea salt water, ruining not only crops but also the soil, and forcing many farmers to emigrate. Now nature amplified such devastating fury.

The *Ramp* killed two thousand people in a country of just over ten million. Scores were buried without being identified. More than seventy thousand people required evacuation. Farms and buildings were ruined. Thousands of farm animals died. It was four years before I was born, but I still heard a lot about it, just as I heard much about the Second World War. Furthermore, this flooding and the lost farmland, buildings, and cattle, also spurred another immigration surge.

Special offerings were taken in churches, even in Canada, for disaster victims and recovery efforts. *De Ramp*, published the same year as the flood, was a commemorative volume sold as a fundraiser for relief efforts. It included a foreword by Queen Juliana, a facsimile of her handwritten letter. The gray and black cover captured my attention first. Front and back showed a large photo of violent waves, the ripples resembling the mottled glass of Opa's living room door. In the water, a horse and cow wade near bushes that are almost completely submerged. Water surges over a bridge, its high rails protruding above the deluge, a rising river inundating its surroundings.

I paged through, ignoring the Dutch text but finding the photos—at least one on every page—fascinating. I studied city streets awash in water. People piling sandbags, clothes and hair tugged and torn by wild winds. Waves sloshing against buildings and through windows, either broken or opened. Grim refugees in flight, wading with blankets or babies in their arms. Immersed gravestones. Dirty bedraggled folks crowded in shelters, trying to sleep. Soldiers and civilians assisting as survivors climb from upper floor windows. The aftermath showed collapsed edifices and furniture scattered on streets. A devastated greenhouse range stood, twisted into ruin, its huge panes swept into the water.

This was no distant disaster in faraway places that I might not have heard of before, where no one I knew had traveled. This happened to people *like us*, with names like Teun and Ton, Bep and Bets, Hetty and Hanny and Henny, Ineke and Dineke and Tineke, Joop and Jaap, Kees and Koos, Wessel and Bessel. They ate *kaas* and *rode kool*, cheese and red cabbage. In a two-page photo, a close friend's father, Bill Suk, was one of a half dozen marines in rain gear crowded into a small boat, rescuing civilians.

The photos that most captivated me, the destinations toward which I paged, showed bloated black and white cows on their sides in mud, others of horses in similar straits. Dead cattle winched onto barges for disposal. I lingered on the ugly images, feeling shame, as if viewing something that I was not supposed to see, drawing my attention but filling me with unease. I looked around to see if adults observed my focused attention. I always noticed suffering.

≡≡

From the Depression, to the Second World War and the Occupation, to the excruciating reconstruction of a ruined economy, to the *Ramp*, the Dutch endured trauma after trauma. And all these only during the twentieth century. No wonder that survival was a prevailing motivator for our immigrants. No wonder they feared so much.

Was anyone ever safely havened? Sorrow is thick throughout Dutch history. Long before Nazis, the country was occupied by Napoleon and before that by the Spanish. Many died during the 1918 influenza epidemic. Hazards are reflected in common sayings. When a room alive with conversational hilarity suddenly falls silent, people comment, *Daar gaat een dominee voorbij*, "There goes a pastor passing by." Not because ministers are necessarily killjoys opposing fun. Rather, in that maritime setting, ministers were officially responsible to inform folks when loved ones drowned or went missing at sea. You hoped never to have a pastor suddenly at your door.

The Dutch have long been flooded with trauma, a culture and a history all too accustomed to bad news.

THIRTEEN

My mother frequently warned me about the Welland Canal, her greatest fear.

That waterway and its boats with flags from around the world fascinated us. Neighborhood boys and girls frequently approached its rounded concrete banks to fish, skip stones, or holler up to sailors on ships, asking them to toss down foreign coins. I was not allowed such things, however. I was not supposed to go near the water. Our family was strict about this too.

One afternoon, chattering children headed toward the canal, passing our house. I watched from under our front yard's leafy chestnut. I recognized Lena, an Italian girl my age who lived around the corner. "They pulled out a drowned man," she called. "We want to see."

I ran and asked my mother's permission to go, just this once. But no. I'm not sure what nightmares a drowned corpse might have sparked. Still it was an exclusion and that was what I felt most keenly.

My mother reminded me again and again to stay away from the canal, especially on the way to and from school.

Broadway Avenue was the longest stretch of my kindergarten commute. A number of properties on both sides of the road had been expropriated by the St. Lawrence Seaway Commission in advance of widening the canal, a project that never did happen. Over our years living in Port Weller, the empty houses deteriorated and collapsed. One by one, their windows were smashed.

Broadway curved upward just before the bridge, along a fence. On the other side of the chain link, land sloped precipitously, nearly vertical, to a concrete channel that drained excess liquid from the lock. Ferocious and turbulent waves bounced and galloped.

"Never go on the other side of that fence," Mom told me. Often. Almost every day.

Once I started home after my morning in kindergarten, gripping a sheet of orange construction paper, a drawing of my father building a greenhouse, something I was eager to show him and hang up, perhaps on the fridge. But a gust of wind tore it loose and dropped it just over the fence.

Sure that I could reach it, I lay on the ground and stretched my arm under the chain links. That did not quite work, so I moved closer, easing my right shoulder underneath, straining.

"Artur!" my mother shouted. It was one of the rare occasions when she'd decided to surprise me on my walk. She grabbed my left arm, yanked me away from the fence and onto my feet, and before jeering schoolmates, walloped my backside. "I told you never to go on the other side."

"But—." Hoping to explain I was not planning to go all the way, just to reach the drawing.

"Never mind."

We walked home in silence. I was sent to bed without supper.

=≡=

My grandmother made money by cleaning mansions overlooking the Niagara River, second homes for wealthy Americans who fussily ran white gloves over mantles and behind knickknacks to check her work. They also gave her liquor store boxes stuffed with cast-offs and hand-me-downs. I do not remember receiving new clothes until junior high.

My mother found a beat-up coat among the loot. She and Tante Joyce turned it inside out and reworked it. The black wool lining, now the exterior, reminded me of fur. I loved its embrace and called it my "bear coat." I would be sorry to outgrow it.

One day, when I was nearly eight, I walked home and studied the woods on my left, scheming and fantasizing about climbing trees, hideouts, Robin Hood adventures. But this forest ran along the canal and was off limits.

Perhaps I could get away with it this once though, I thought. No one need know. I wanted to approach that water.

I looked around, and seeing myself alone I pushed through bushes, came to the concrete embankment, and studied the mottled brown-green water flowing north to Lake Ontario, a half mile away. I moved along in the same direction as the current. I picked up a branch, a forked piece of timber as long as I was tall, and used it as a walking stick. I whacked weeds, wielding it as a sword against imaginary opponents. Finally I jettisoned it through the air into the water, hoping to spear a sea monster.

After twenty minutes of wandering and exploring, I emerged from the brush and noticed something that sped my heart—burrs covered my coat. It was obvious that I had been in the neighborhood's only forest. My parents were going to know.

I sat beside the road and tried to pick out the prickles, but there were too many—hundreds of Velcro barbs that resisted removal. Each tug left telltale accusations. I could not clean this coat and to keep trying would make me get home late, another punishable offense.

So I strategized, not wanting to wait for Mom to discover what I had done. I decided to preemptively confess and suggest a remedy, hoping to avoid having my rump whacked by the *mattenklopper* or wooden spoon.

I entered as usual through the back door into the kitchen and found her preparing supper, her back turned to me.

"How was your day?"

"I got to tell you something."

She turned, a question on her face, then her eyes swivelled to brown barbs embedded in black faux fur.

"I did something bad." My words tumbled faster as her face reddened. "I walked through the woods. That's how I got these prickers. Can I clean my coat for my punishment?"

She agreed and set me up on a kitchen chair in the garage, its large door propped open. I did not get afternoon cookies and milky tea that day. The family ate supper, watching me through the dining room window. I was not permitted to eat. Finally, around 7 p.m., almost bedtime, my mother came out, offered to finish the cleanup, and sent me to brush my teeth and get into pajamas.

The next morning, my stomach gurgling from hunger, I saw my bear coat hanging by the back door, burr-free. The incident reminds me of my stern upbringing, and I question the harshness of no supper. Still, I understand my parents' leeriness of the canal—every year people drowned. I am impressed that my mother accepted my proposed punishment and that she finally relieved me by taking care of my coat. I learned the lesson they wanted to impress on me. In seven years of living within a few hundred yards of the canal, that was the only time I ventured to its side without an adult. I am also struck now by how obedient I usually was, a mostly compliant child. Unlike my father, I lived in fear of doing something wrong, stepping amiss, always afraid of being punished, meeting their disapproval. Much like I fretted about disobeying God and the consequences of that.

≕

Mostly, God was someone to be feared. I heard that in church, one of the few things I understood from sermons. God peered down from on high, waiting for one misstep or one doctrine going amiss. Sundays were solemn.

Not until high school when I began visiting friends' churches did I realize that worship could be fun. That one could rip into rousing songs and roar their lyrics. That one could laugh—even during sermons.

And later than that, I learned from theologians such as Henri Nouwen that faith could be about joy, not just duty and fear of punishment for disobedience. That God is about blessing and empowering. That God wants brokenness and woundedness healed. That God wants us whole.

That one could trust God.

A close friend's son is no longer a believer, even though he was raised in the church. The son asked his preacher dad whether he was worried that his son might go to hell. The dad responded: "I know how much I love you, how crazy I am about you, just because I am your father. Imagine. God created you. How much greater must God's love be for you. I trust you in God's hands." I do not blame Maranatha Christian Reformed or Calvin Memorial Christian School, but I did not hear such sentiments in either of those places.

And now, for thirty years or more, whenever anyone asks me—either as a pastor or priest or as a Christian friend—for prayer or a blessing, I usually end the petition for someone with words like these: "May you always know deep in your heart how much God loves you."

One especially cold winter day, the Lock One bridge remained tipped up into the sky. We saw this sight often in summer but seldom in winter. For those few cold months we did not worry about the bridge rising when planning a trip to St. Catharines because in winter no boats passed. (The rest of the year we always left extra early for appointments because the bridge could go up at any time and we might have to wait for twenty minutes or more.) In December, the canal was drained for inspection, repairs, and maintenance on lock systems and bridges. Bikes, cars, corpses, and occasional skeletons were recovered from the exposed mud at the bottom.

The crossing guard, Mr. Watkins—I thought of him as *Mr. Walkins* since he protected us walkers—gathered children on the sidewalk. He lived two blocks from our house. Knowing that my family was Dutch, he regularly told me that as a World War II soldier he guarded the Ottawa Civic Hospital room where Dutch Princess Juliana gave birth to Princess Margriet.*

Mr. Watkins said, "Kids, the bridge is up for repairs and won't come down today. All traffic has to go around to the next Lock. I'll help you across."

I had a dilemma. My mother told me often that I was never allowed near the canal. I hesitantly followed him; what else could I do? I was also supposed to obey authority figures or else my parents—and God—would be angry. Our group climbed down a metal stairway into gloppy mud at the bottom and moved over a frozen stream. We passed gingerly on the glassy surface, wondering whether it would hold. Canadian children slide feet slowly on ice, listening for cracks. Even if someone ahead safely passes over a spot, one is never sure. He or she may damage the ice. Crossing the canal was not quite a Jesus-grade walking-on-water miracle, and not quite the "I walked and sank not on the storm-vexed sea" of the hymn "I Sought the Lord," but it was an exceptional experience nonetheless.

---

* *Princess Margriet*: During World War II, most of the Dutch royal family went into exile in England. Princess Juliana lived in Canada where Margriet was born. People liked to say that her hospital room was temporarily declared Dutch territory. This birth endeared Canada to the Dutch, one reason that many Dutch emigrants chose Canada as a destination. After the war, the Dutch gratefully gave a hundred thousand tulip bulbs to Ottawa and continued to send thousands yearly ever since.

I was too worried, however, about possibly breaking a rule to enjoy this opportunity. The possibility of sin lurked.

I felt anxious about confessing all this to my mom, unsure whether I had done right or whether I would be punished for improvisational infraction.

At home, she had her ironing board set up in the living room, where she watched a soap opera—*The Edge of Night*, I believe—as she worked. Normally, she sent us to another part of the house until it ended because of adult-oriented content. I moved quietly beside her.

My mom entranced, I watched too. A couple, both apparently married to other people, shared a tender moment. The dark-haired man told the blond woman, "Your eyes are like a mirror. I see my reflection in them."

"The eyes are windows to the soul, honey," she said.

I often looked for myself in the eyes of others.

FOURTEEN

When I was in my early sixties, a Dutch relative, a successful entrepreneur and cousin of my father, hosted a reunion of Great-grandfather Pleun's descendants. Astonishingly, he funded the entire enterprise, including flying people from the Netherlands, Ontario, and Oregon, to gather for a weeklong cruise on the Danube. Around two hundred people accepted the invitation. He paid for the cruise, entertainment and tours, food and refreshments, and massive volumes of champagne to celebrate New Year's Eve in Vienna.

In preparation he sought biographies of all Pleun's descendants. I wrote mine as well as entries about my closest Boers relatives who had died: sister Margaret, my father Pleun, Opa Arie. I had plenty of material. But I knew that a reunion book was *not* the place to describe or raise questions about generational patterns of abuse, alcohol, or anger, even though I was surely not the only one in the family tree so afflicted.

Families teach us limits, often without giving us explicit directions about what we tell others. As a child I knew, as if by osmosis, which complaints not to discuss outside the home. I wondered whether the reunion might be an occasion for people to talk informally about family wounds. But that didn't happen during our time together, at least not within my hearing.

Ancestors who came from the Glazen Stad learned not to throw stones, not to ask questions, living as we did in and with glass houses. All families have secrets.

≕≔

I always felt uncomfortable looking into the face of a boyhood friend, Barry, because his left cornea was badly scarred, its blue crisscrossed with zigzag white lines, his eye a smashed pane. Sometimes his brothers whispered that a window broke above Barry's crib when he was a baby and flying glass tore up his eyeball. I accepted that sad story at face value.

Now I wonder how that window broke.

Families can be rough, families at home, and families of faith.

⇒⇐

Our church proclaimed two major ethical injunctions, standards to measure faithfulness and church respectability.

The first commandment loomed large. *Remember the Sabbath day by keeping it holy.* We heard all Ten Commandments every Sunday near the beginning of the service, but this one got special attention. Most of us spent no money that day as that would make others work. Gas for the car and milk and bread for the family were to be purchased by Saturday. Some of us could ride bikes or romp outside on Sunday, some could not. My friend Bernie was not allowed to remove his church suit or change into everyday clothes. He could sit on the porch but not play in the yard. Our family did not go to restaurants or the cinema that day because that required spending money and thus forcing others to work. Of course some never went to the cinema at all; some did not even own a televsion. We all honored the Sabbath in some way. Even my type A father did, a counterbalance to his workaholism.

But our family fell short on Sabbath holiness because ministers often reminded us to attend church *twice*, in the morning and then late afternoon. Our family did not, going only in the morning, and I, pious as I already was becoming, felt relief. Once seemed ample. My parents commented that this violation meant we would always remain fringe members.

The second commandment, like unto it, was equally emphatic. *Thou shalt send thy children to Christian school.* There were subtexts. Not any Christian school, but *ours*, our form of *Dutch Calvinism*, Christian Reformed to be exact—Calvin Memorial Christian School, grades one through eight, on Scott Street, directly across from our church.*

* *Sectarian institutions*: In the Netherlands, liberal Calvinists, conservative Calvinists, Roman Catholics, and secular groups each had their own schools, printing

The young teachers, few with teacher training, were from our church. All students had Dutch names. One or two were a slightly less strict stripe of Calvinism, but that was it for diversity. For years, "Christian" and "Christian Reformed"* were precise equivalents in my mind. Sometimes my tongue slipped and I called our school "Calvin Memorial Christian *Reformed*," much to the amusement of public school children in my neighborhood, who taunted: "Figures! A *reform* school!"

Calvin students lined up outdoors four times a day—before school began, when lunch was over, and at the end of morning and afternoon recess. Fellow first-grader Chip, with his curly brown hair, ready smile, and cruel instincts, always pushed in behind me. He and I both wore clumsy ankle-covering orthopedic boots to correct flat feet; we both had calloused left thumbs from inadvertent nighttime sucking. But we had little else in common.

"Hey, Boers, you stink today."

"What a stupid lunch pail. Stripes? Look at mine. Flintstones!"

Sometimes he slapped the back of my head or pulled my hair, then gig-

---

presses, unions, political parties, graveyards. Dutch people—religious or secular—existed almost entirely within their own sectarian context. My mother remembers that members of the mainline Calvinist church in the Netherlands and members of her orthodox Calvinist church were discouraged from dating one another, let alone marrying.

In Canada Christian Reformed immigrants also developed their own specific institutions: schools (first grade schools, then high schools, colleges, and a graduate institution), labor unions, farmer's federations, newspapers, political advocacy organizations, retirement and nursing homes. The first priority, though, after churches were established and built, was grade schools.

* *Dutch Calvinist schisms*: Christian Reformed was the largest Dutch denomination among Canadian immigrants; it was the best organized in welcoming and integrating immigrants. Most Dutch Protestant immigrants did not join Canadian churches but went to ones established by their compatriots or began their own. We were annoyed when others confused our name. People still ask me whether I grew up "Dutch Reformed." The confusion is understandable. There is no contemporary denomination named "Dutch Reformed," but rather many forms of Dutch Calvinism. In the Netherlands and North America, Dutch Calvinists are prone to schism. Besides Christian Reformed, other immigrants might belong to the Reformed Church of America, the Canadian Reformed Church (equivalent of Article 31 or Liberated), Free Christian Reformed, Free Reformed, Protestant Reformed, Orthodox Protestant Reformed, and Netherlands Reformed. In recent decades emerging configurations include the Orthodox Christian Reformed, Independent Christian Reformed, and Independent Reformed.

gled. Sometimes he yanked my jacket. I tried timing my line arrival to avoid him, but he inevitably inserted himself behind me.

My one response, over and again, "Leave me alone!"

He never did.

I complained over supper, evening after evening.

"Today Chip kicked me in the back of my knee."

"Chip shoved me so hard that I banged into Alice, and then she was mad at me."

"Chip hit me with his bag of marbles."

One night after supper, my father brought me to the living room, sat down on the couch, stood me in front of him, lit a cigarette, and said: "Son, there is only one way to deal with a bully."

"What?"

"Fight him."

"I don't want to. He'd win."

"You have to try. Here, let me show you. Make a fist with your right hand."

I tried to imitate what he demonstrated.

"No. Don't put your thumb inside your fingers. Keep it outside."

I adjusted.

"OK, that's good. You've got a fist." He extended his hand, palm outward, toward me. "Punch this as hard as you can."

I obeyed, although this went against the grain—striking adults a serious offense.

"Do it again. Harder."

This next attempt staggered me.

"OK, one more time. Spread your feet. Keep your balance."

And again, grunting as I swung. Knuckles stinging.

"Good job. Now here's what you do. When Chip bothers you, make a fist, go fast and surprise him, hit him here," pointing to the bridge of his nose. "That spot hurts. He'll stop picking on you." I dreamed for a moment of what I'd seen on TV where enemies with glass chins immediately fell to the ground, knocked out.

When the first bell clanged the next day, I took my place and my friend Larry arrived behind me. Chip, though, soon shoved in between: "I want to stand here."

"Hey, Boers, I bet your mom put garbage in your lunch today."

I bunched my right hand, turned around to my left, and swung against his nose. His eyes widened uncertainly and then spurted water. Howling, he covered his face with his right hand.

"Leave me alone, Chip."

And he did. From then on he was friendly. Years later, even when we were in our late teens, he occasionally asked, "Remember when you punched me?"

After that experience, I easily took offense and was quick to launch my fist. If boys kicked in reaction, I'd step back and catch their ascending leg and twist my enemy to the ground, another trick learned from my father. Sometimes that was enough. Sometimes I then sat on them, slapping faces or punching chests. I was proud that I could physically best—wrestling or punching—most boys in my grade.

After I walked a mile, crossed the bridge, and waited by a streetlight, my bus ride took an hour and a half—even though the school was only three miles away. We served a wide area; our bus wound all over the county, crawling over its long route, ours the only Christian Reformed school for dozens of miles, from Niagara-on-the Lake to Port Weller to Port Dalhousie, even to Louth Township.

I hated that commute. Jouncing through potholes. Noisy antics of schoolmates. Clammy heat of crammed bodies. Sour puke fumes lingering and drifting for days, no matter how much sawdust the driver tossed on the floor.

Besides, buses could be terrifying.

Ours hit black ice one morning, careened and bounced through a deep ditch, swayed precariously through an unmown field without toppling, and finally jerked to a rest four feet short of a peach tree. Students were uninjured, just shaken. The next day we had a new driver.

After school another winter day, pupils scrambled around the gravel parking lot, hurrying to get to their rides. Two blond-braided girls fell while running on the snow and slid together under a moving bus, its exhaust pipe emitting puffs of gray plumes into Arctic air. A rear wheel rolled over their legs and they began screaming. I and other onlookers did too, expecting guts to spurt yellow and red. Astonishingly, they were unhurt, the vehicle passing over their thighs, merely pressing them deeper into the unplowed snow. They crawled, stood, brushed their red nylon snowpants, and walked away. Crying, but unhurt, almost a miracle.

Still, when I got home a couple hours later, I could not stop my arms and legs from trembling. "I'm silly," I told my mother. "They weren't hurt."

But she was more empathetic. "No, not silly. You're in shock." She held me in her lap beside the warm living room radiator, in front of the bay window. My body gradually quieted.

One day a temporary school bus driver, not knowing the route, raced by as I waited at my stop. Schoolmates pressed noses against panes, pointed, blew raspberries, and hollered through windows, "See you, Boers. Nya nya." I walked the three miles to school, consoling myself by picking up empty pop bottles from ditches, hoping to cash glass for deposits, one of the few ways to get spending money. I stuffed them into my lunch bag and pockets, too many to carry by hand. At school, my teacher reprimanded my tardiness and confiscated the treasured finds.

Another time I arrived at my stop in a blizzard—mittens on, scarf around my face, parka hood over my head—and waited an hour in hurtling snow that stung my exposed cheeks like tiny glass shards. Finally I gave up and returned home, my feet numb from cold. My mother made phone calls and learned that buses had been cancelled that day because of weather. No one had informed us. She held me again beside the living room radiator for a long time, trying to melt my toes and fingertips.

That bus commute taught other status lessons.

I walked along Broadway Avenue before crossing the Lock One Bridge. The bus could easily have diverted to a diagonal street, a quarter mile along the Seaway Haulage Road, and cut my journey in half, adding a minute or two to its route. When I occasionally suggested this to my parents over supper, they told me that our family, on the congregation's fringes, would never get such service.

But the pastor's children were picked up right after me. For them, the bus went a mile out of the way to a quiet residential side street and stopped directly in front of their house. Of the dozens of riders, they were the only ones to receive door-to-door privileges.

I seldom knew where to sit on those commutes. Certainly not beside girls because then boys taunted about "cooties." Most boys parked lunch pails beside themselves, "saving" spots.

Fortunately Henry Vriend, soft-spoken with a gentle smile, often had room. He lived around the corner from my Opa and Oma in Niagara-on-the-Lake. When we visited them I would walk to his house to play. He was not a close friend, but a reliable acquaintance. I felt a measure of safety beside him.

Still, it was not enough to mind one's business or quietly converse with a seatmate. Other boys strutted up and down the aisle, banging seats and flinging insults. Sometimes in the morning they snagged my lunch, dangling it just beyond my reach before sliding down a bus window and pitching my food onto passing pavement. On cold afternoons they treated my woollen balaclava similarly. I ran through lots of hats, not only on the bus.

Once, outside at school, older pupils surrounded me, pulled my hat from my head for "Monkey in the Middle." I frantically charged from tormentor to tormentor, demanding, "Give me that!" until one threw it high onto the school's flat roof. Laughing, the group dispersed. I reported this to the office; a custodian got out a ladder and retrieved my hat. No teacher or official followed up with the students.

Similarly, in grade three I entered the washroom and a group of grade six students nabbed my hat, tossed it into a tall white urinal, and predictably anointed it. When they left I gingerly retrieved and rinsed it, trying not to vomit. Wearing it home later that day (I knew I was not allowed to go outside without my hat), I thought about Al Bertrand's piss lingering close to my scalp.

Nothing about the *Lord of the Flies* felt surprising when I read it a few years later in grade nine.

=⇒⇐=

Christian school students excelled at humiliation.

I barely recall the most intense experience. Two or three dozen pupils surrounded and taunted me in the yard near the baseball diamond. I can't remember what they said or what prompted the razzing. The more visibly upset I became, the harder they laughed. A teacher finally broke up that interaction and escorted me to my classroom to await the end of lunch hour.

I was not the only one afflicted. Bullying was rife there. Half a century later, other students remember that the schoolyard and the buses were frightening locations of intimidation and harassment. Once my sister started school, she too was hounded. When pupils on the bus or in the schoolyard harassed her, I walked up and administered my father's bully prescription.

And now I wonder. What made us targets? Did we have provocative behavioral tics? Did they sense in us ready-made victims?

Bullies show up everywhere, inflicting and perpetuating pain.

Hadn't Margaret and I snipped our kittens' whiskers? And forced them into dolls' clothes and a doll's high chair? In the summer, hadn't we dropped them into our plastic wading pool, to watch their panicked explosion from water? And on a snowy day, hadn't we juggled them outside until the tiny creatures trembled from fear and cold?

⇒⇐

One Sunday, seven years old, I tossed a swing back and forth with my four-year-old sister. She turned and I launched the seat, aiming to startle her. Instead, its corner caught her cheek. "Uh oh," I thought, not just out of concern for her. I escorted her to the house where our parents entertained relatives in the living room. Margaret's howls heralded our approach.

Once she and I made it into the dining room, my father, still in church suit and tie, surged up. Anger rippled his features. Seeing her bleeding cheek, he asked nothing. I felt light-headed. My groin clenched, my stomach contracted. I wanted to explain, calm him, plead.

"But—," I began, and his fist flew.

I remember these things clearly: cool sunny day, shredded clouds scudding in the sky, the blue-flowered pattern on Margaret's white dress, her parted blond hair and indigo barrettes. I see her startled shock at my bone-headed play. The long walk from the swing set, across the yard, through the house. I hear my one-word objection and see his raised fist.

And then, nothing.

Hours later, I woke in my parents' bed, sore, worn out, aching. That I remember. The Sunday visitors treated me circumspectly, like a convalescent. Over a supper of tomato soup and cold cut sandwiches, we discussed the weather and school the next day. No one mentioned events in that very dining room a few hours earlier. I pondered them alone. No one looked at me. I somehow knew that what happened was not to be discussed. I never told anyone about it. The shame was mine and mine alone to carry. Only now that I am in my sixties do I begin to share these things, and I often feel shocked at the evident shock of others when I do. Shock at the violence or shock at violating the implicit family rule not to talk about such things.

I still puzzle at that memory gap between my father's looming approach and then my waking in their room.

Once, after I was well into adulthood, my mother mentioned this incident. "I didn't know what to do. Your father was going crazy, and I was scared. Your uncle helped me pull him off you. Then we laid you in bed." I want more details but now she hardly remembers.

Before my father died, I tried to discuss this assault with my parents—me in my mid-thirties and my father knowing that his cancer was terminal.

My mom said, "That's why I usually did the punishing. We couldn't trust his temper."

Pa said only, "You were stupid; you could have killed your sister."

Could he have killed me?

Adults didn't apologize, even though they regularly ordered children to do so, telling us, "Say you're sorry."

I often was.

FIFTEEN

Sundays we wore our best clothes, greeted other Dutch immigrants before worship, and visited with them afterward in the parking lot. Men dug cigarettes from jacket pockets and shared lighters or passed packs of matches, flames flickering in front of their faces. *Lucifers* is the Dutch word for "matches."

Women fiddled with purses, swaying slightly on high heels to stay balanced atop gravel. Kids scuffed gently at the gray stones, not daring to mess polished Sunday shoes. Adults commented on the ironies of weather: "This year we had a white Easter and a green Christmas."

After church in the car I often complained, "I couldn't understand the minister. He used big words." I was sure that he'd said important things, and I wanted to be included, just as I wanted to know what adults laughed about over their coffee or cocktails. On those occasions, I could just pretend and laugh anyway. But sermons did not work that way for me.

"Wait till you're older," my father responded.

Smoke from his Buckinghams pooled against the glass, making everything hazy.

≡≡

I anticipated God showing up in splendor at any moment, hoping he'd arrive before the bomb dropped or communists took over, two threats I regularly heard about at dinner and when company visited. At school, we practiced duck-and-cover, huddling under desks, in case of an atom bomb. "Turn your faces from the windows," our teachers admonished. Glass could easily become shrapnel after all. Every week our congregation recited that Jesus "will come again to judge the living and the dead." I expected this in my lifetime, possibly within weeks. I would see it. Our church's name, "Maranatha," invited his return; I liked that.

After coming back from church in our bulbous four-door olive green Chevrolet, I climbed from the backseat, my father's smoke billowing out around me. I stepped onto our gravel driveway, beside our tattered red Insulbrick house, I in a navy blue hand-me-down sailor's suit, given to my grandmother by wealthy Americans. Turning my face to cobalt sky and glaring sun, I checked. Jesus might float down at this very moment, beyond the widely arched chestnut branches in our front yard, arms uplifted, calf-deep in bulky clouds. It would probably occur on a Sunday I was sure, right after we had done our duty by going to church, acknowledging our faithful attendance, and before the unnecessary second service, and I would be among the first special ones to notice. I was happy to be in on God's plans, not entirely sure why I got to be part of that special circle.

Or, maybe I did think I deserved it.

＝＝

For a time, I believed in Saint Nicholas—*Sinterklaas*. And in fairies, hoping for a dime as I nested teeth under my pillow. When our family drove to Maine to visit relatives, Mom told me a "fairy" would carry us across Lake Champlain. How large she must be to lift a car, I thought, picturing gossamer wings the size of tall sails. On the car-laden ship I asked, "Where's the fairy?" and then learned a new word in my second language.

On that same trip, my parents took us to a small amusement park, a Santa's Village, his home away from the North Pole we were told. It was September, the school year had begun, and not many other families wandered the grounds. Being there was a treat; we were special.

I remember small wooden chalets, white splotched paint emulating snow. We petted reindeer, marvelling at how small they were, feeding them pellets purchased by inserting pennies into gumball machines topped with glass astronaut helmets.

We paused in an open building constructed of thick dark beams and watched an old-fashioned blacksmith wearing a thick leather apron strike his blackened anvil with a heavy hammer. He laid two horseshoe nails in flames until they glowed red, then used tongs to bend them into circles. Water steamed and sizzled as he dropped them in a bucket.

A few minutes later, he presented us with rings, Margaret and I surprised that he knew our size. Each of us slid one on a finger. Driving away, she and I fiddled with our prizes in the back seat, with plump Oma who was visiting from the Netherlands between us.

Zijn ze niet gevaarlijk?, asked my grandmother: "Aren't they dangerous?" *Ik geloof dat ze lood zin.* "I believe they are lead."

My mother turned, held out her hand: "Give them. I want to see."

Obediently pulling them off, we laid them on her palm. "What's wrong, Mom?" I asked.

Saying nothing she extended them to my father, who glanced from behind the wheel. "Yeah, they look like lead."

My mother turned. "Lead is dangerous. What if you put these in your mouth?"

"We won't, Mom. Promise."

"No, it's too risky. We need to get rid of them."

"Please, Mom, no."

"But—."

"No arguments."

She rolled down her window. As our car sped down the secondary highway, she tossed the mementos toward the white pines and silver birches whirring by.

⸻

One summer day I played with neighborhood kids, including frizzy redheaded Robin, such a Canadian name. She was the first stranger I'd ever kissed. It was a week earlier, ducked between hedges beside the driveway. Our teeth collided, and I tasted peanut butter.

The group declared the urgent importance of leaping onto a deck without using stairs. Maybe it was a boat and we were drowning in grass, perhaps a castle to shelter us from rampaging dragons, possibly escape from pursuing Nazis. The others quickly made it to safety. I could not.

"Arthur! Hurry!" they urged. The more anxious their voices, the less able I felt. I could not lift myself, could not swing my legs up and around.

I panicked at the impending terror—drowning or dragons or Nazis—and felt frustration. I already knew that I was not as physically adept as others who batted balls, jumped high, ran bases.

"Here," Robin called, safely atop the platform of weathered two-by-fours. She tugged from her arm an elastic bracelet strung with plastic gewgaws and stretched it toward me. "Wear my lucky charms."

I slipped it over my wrist and jumped onto the wood. "Wow," I said. "What happened?"

"Charms help you do stuff."

Next time at the A&P grocery, I paused in front of the tall plate windows next to the doors and begged for a nickel to put in a bubble gum machine. Looking through the spherical glass I wanted to acquire charms.

"That's wasting money," my mother told me.

"But they helped me jump and climb."

"That's superstition. We don't believe that."

Santa Claus, fairies and ferries, and lucky charms did not preoccupy me for long. Most beliefs dissipated. Shopping mall Santas made me suspicious. Such variation, some bespectacled and others not. Warren, the boy next door, explained that "tooth fairies" were parents.

But God dwelled within me differently. God would not be dislodged.

I trusted our church. Our minister would not lie; he was chosen by God and spoke for God. Parents did not make the sun rise, stars dot skies and sparkle at night, or bunnies bounce from bushes.

＝＝

I always believed in God.

And believed nothing could be more important. Nothing outweighed staying on God's good side, especially since ministers and Christian school teachers and my parents frightened me when they spoke of hell and eternal flames. I longed for God's approval.

I thought about God, what God was like, what God wanted. I began to direct ideas, thoughts, and feelings God's way. This seemed an obvious thing to do. To others, I talked about God. A lot. Most people went to church. Most, I assumed, believed in God. Surely, most would want to discuss him. Might even be interested in what I knew about God.

But Mom and Papa complained about church "fanatics" with *overdreven,* "exaggerated," "put on," faith, who sat in front pews trying to befriend the minister. We were not like that, they reminded me.

I didn't find much interest with other people either. A cousin raved about the Maple Leafs. Johnny and Ricky fondly recounted the achievements of their new beagle, Pokey. Warren played with the massive Tonka tow truck he received for Christmas (causing me, I admit, to wonder why Dutch people did not, as my parents explained, "spoil" kids with expensive gifts).

But mostly my attention was elsewhere. On other realities.

I did not ask to long for God. Yet nothing draws me more, even now. Some days I examine my ambitions and whether there is still time to achieve them as I have long passed sixty. Some days I can't shake crushes and infatuations, my attention drawn by new women I meet, in the grocery store or at a conference. I wonder whether such longings ever disappear. Some days I just want to play card games online. But every day, many times each day, I pine for God, address God; God is never far from my thoughts and concerns. A safe haven for my fears and longings.

Over the decades, I occasionally felt God's presence, for a time when I was a young adult as a burning in my chest. Sometimes I had an inspired dream, now and then an insight from seemingly nowhere—a voice or almost a voice, as when God called me during the missionary's presentation. Those encounters always made me want more such experiences, made me want them always.

⇒⇐

Walking home from grade school, bundled in a padded coat, my throat wrapped in a thick scarf knit by my mother, woollen hat clasping my head, I noticed baby Jesus in the bay window of a house a few blocks from ours. Dazzling snow lay deep, squeaking under my rubber galoshes, not the usual setting for biblical scenes, not as I'd heard them after dinner at the dining room table or at church in Sunday school. Yet there he was, manger baby, enraptured parents, scattered straw, colorful characters. In cheek-biting wind, I went closer, standing still before the frosted pane, snow coming to the upper edge of my galoshes, my breath steaming onto the glass and then erratically freezing there.

Each day I paused to ponder beside that picture window. When I finally told my mother, she said, "Oh, that's a nativity. Catholics do that, not us." Graven images again. Yet she arranged an idol visit. My parents knew the family, also Dutch immigrants. I trudged through the snow for an examination, this time from inside the house. Mrs. Tuinder served hot chocolate and allowed me to touch the figurines.

A dozen years later, my sister—she had leukemia by then—would buy a small nativity scene that could be plugged in and lit with a Christmas tree bulb, the first time I ever saw a Protestant-owned creche. I would finally purchase my own when I was thirty, desiring our children to have one.

⇒⇐

Wanting my folks, teachers, and friends' parents to like me, I strove to figure out rules, to be polite. I liked to think that after I visited Ricky and Johnny, Ludolph or Gary, their fathers and mothers would say, "What a nice boy." Maybe adding, "Why can't you be more like him?"

I worried about going wrong and fretted about hell. Sundays in church our *Dominee* recited the Ten Commandments: "I the Lord thy God am a jealous God." I might fail God's rules, perhaps get things hurled at me by God, just as my father hurled things. I didn't understand sermons, but I knew doctrine had to be correct, had to be Reformed. If I got my beliefs wrong, I would not have any appeal or argument with God, just as I never did with my dad. It would be all over. And the flames eternal.

I fretted about the spiritual well-being of friends. Like Hendrine and Peter who went to see Disney's *That Darn Cat!* I was shocked by that title's expletive and shocked that their parents let them go. And shocked by how enthusiastically they recounted the film's plot and repeated the film's title. I wondered whether their souls were damaged.

⇒⇐

To the east of Calvin Memorial Christian School sat a small white clapboard building, originally built by Dutch immigrants, one of the Niagara Peninsula's first Christian Reformed churches. There, my parents wed, and there my sister and I were baptized as babies, in a small frilly gown cut from my mother's wedding dress. With a steady influx of immigrants, and babies produced by immigrants, our congregation outgrew that facility in a few years, sold it to Seventh-day Adventists, and built a larger structure across the road. Adventists mystified me. Why go to church on Saturday? Who wants that?

After school one day I walked through the parking lot and stopped halfway to the street, on the spot where we played red rover at recess. Children chattered and scattered, running past, toward lined-up buses, gleeful about another day's end, taunting, "Last one there. . . ."

The school behind me, our church before me across the road, the erring Adventist structure beside me, I thought about how we Christian Reformed, of all believers, understood God best of all—honoring Sundays, saying prayers before and after meals, going to Christian schools. Why I was fortunate to be among the chosen I had no idea, but I remembered fancy terms that teachers said in class and that the minister pronounced in sermons: "elect," "predestined." Words heard nowhere else. The minister often told us that baby baptism meant we were all in God's covenant.

"Thank you," I whispered, never doubting our unique belovedness. Just as God had a chosen people in the Old Testament, God had a chosen people now: us Dutch Calvinists. When I was growing up, our private school was Calvin Memorial Christian School, Calvinettes were our church's version of Girl Scouts while the boys joined Calvinist Cadets. Our denominational newspaper was the *Calvinist Contact*, and my best friend was named Calvin (he prefers "Kevin"). I believed myself predestined to go to Calvin College and was confused upon hearing that there was once an American president named Calvin Coolidge.

To be Christian was fine, even good, but Calvinist and thus Christian *Reformed* even better. Among that elite, I felt God's favor and perceived God's warmth and affection, safer than what I received from my dad. We were special, unique. I was special, unique.

Some other Christians, though—these in another small white clapboard building, this one just northwest of our church—gave me pause. During hot weather, our church custodian opened our opaque windows, hoping breezes might cool sticky worshippers; the nearby Pentecostals opened theirs too. They sang and shouted, their joyful noise penetrating our solemnity. When we went outside to our cars after the service, we heard them and their loud rhythms more clearly—clapping, guitars, drums.

My former jazz drummer father and I looked at each other. He smiled, and I knew that we both wanted to clap and join such rousing renditions.

We wanted to be in *that* number, to sway and stomp feet, maybe dance and bounce. Like he and I did when he blared Dixieland on our living room stereo, both of us hollering "Oh, yeah!" as we had learned from Satchmo. Why couldn't we do that in church?

—=≡=—

At Calvin Memorial Christian School we studied the Bible in addition to math and reading. Teachers tested us, and I invented ways to remember Scripture stories and names. Noah's sons were easy. The first was "Ham." I thought of cold cuts. Then "Shem," the Dutch word for "jam," something else for sandwiches, a natural second component. After that, "Japheth" rolled automatically. "Ham, Shem, and Japheth" I repeated to myself over and again as I prepared for a quiz. "Shadrach, Meshach, and Abednego" were a little trickier to recall.

We sang hymns every morning. I particularly loved "Savior, Like a Shepherd Lead Us."

> Savior, like a shepherd lead us
> Much we need Thy tender care
> In Thy pleasant pastures feed us
> For our use Thy folds prepare.
> Blessed Jesus, blessed Jesus
> Thou hast bought us, Thine we are
> Blessed Jesus, blessed Jesus
> Thou hast bought us, Thine we are.

Pupils were required to take turns reading aloud a Bible passage at lunch. At first I had no idea how to choose a text. Then I noticed many psalms were subtitled, "A Psalm of David." That sounded good. I recognized the name. So, when my turn came, I paged through the small black, red-letter King James to the Psalms, easy to find, dead center in the book, and chose one by David, preferably not too long.

—=≡=—

In grade five, Miss DeHaan, with her gaunt bespectacled face, reminded us about how Jesus "bore our sins on the cross." Having recently read *Tom*

Sawyer I recalled that when beautiful Becky—I would have loved her too, her blond locks reminded me of Dorothy—damaged a teacher's book, Tom took the blame, earning a second whipping that day. That was like Jesus! Three times I raised my hand to report this parallel and three times I was called upon and each time I began, "In *Tom Sawyer*," before my teacher cut me off.

"We know you liked that book, Arthur. We're not talking about that now."

"But—."

"Please drop this."

I felt disappointment at not being able to demonstrate my insight. I loved raising my hand to answer the teachers' questions, even if at other times teachers also reminded me to stop looking out the window and day-dreaming. I felt aggrieved by this injustice; she did not recognize my good behavior and my theological cleverness. I wanted to be precocious. I had a sense of the concept, if not the word itself.

≡≡

Calvin Memorial put on Christmas and Easter programs, held in our church across the road. Because of my confident voice I was often given speaking parts, asked to deliver a reading, or even narrate part of the program.

The building filled with dads in suits and ties and mothers in dresses and hats. Our minister, Reverend Geleynse, complimented my enunciation. He, other parents, and some teachers told me the same thing: "Maybe you'll be a minister someday." I felt myself beaming.

Here was an idea. Is that, I wondered, why I felt God moving me, in this very room a few years ago, back when I listened to the missionary telling us about Nigeria? Is a strong reading voice what it takes to be a pastor? Could I be the important person standing behind the high pulpit? Having a whole roomful of people listening to what I had to say, week after week? I hugged these ideas inside, sure that no one else in my class heard the same compliment.

≡≡

In 1967, Canada's Centennial year, my parents paid five dollars and swore allegiance to the Queen. The Canadian Bible Society, "auxiliary of the British and Foreign Bible Society," presented each new citizen with a small King James. My mother passed hers to me. It still sits on my bookshelf.

When I was eleven, I began reading it daily. Starting with Genesis, I dutifully tackled a chapter a day until the end of Revelation and then all over again. I know now that I mispronounced "Job," "Habakkuk," and "Philemon" in my head. King James grammar and vocabulary stymied me at times, but I persisted, day after day, chapter by chapter. Verses that impressed me I underlined with a red pen. I don't know where I got that idea.

Reading in Revelation that only 144,000 would be in heaven, I tried to calculate the average number of people saved annually over two millennia, marvelling at how few of us twentieth-century folk would be there, yet certain I was in that number. I wondered whether I might be one of the two witnesses in the last days described in Revelation, whom God would "grant authority to prophesy for one thousand two hundred sixty days, wearing sackcloth."

I am not sure how I came to this daily Bible reading. Perhaps our minister or a Christian schoolteacher suggested it. No one I knew, family or friends, did this. My parents worried about my being *overdreven*, growing fanatical, one of those annoying people to disparage and dismiss.

SIXTEEN

I was in my late forties, waiting to fall asleep across the ocean in a room crowded with dozens of strangers, all of us in bunk beds, when an unexpected memory surfaced.

I was a pilgrim on Spain's Camino de Santiago, at the end of one more grueling day's hike. After my first week of walking, neither my feet nor my muscles had toughened up enough to match the distance of each daily trek. The sun felt oppressively hot with temperatures reaching over 100 degrees. My backpack was drenched with sweat. I could not drink enough water.

Finally, entering a city of stone buildings and cobbled streets, I trudged into the shelter—legs leaden, blistered feet afire. In the courtyard, bedraggled pilgrims gleefully stripped off shoes and socks, bathing feet in the cold water of a fountain. Later we plodded inside without footwear, the cool surface of smoothly polished slate floors soothing sore soles.

We slept in a large room with fifty numbered bunk beds. The paternalistic hostel keeper assigned each of us to a particular unit. Glad to lie down, I did not much mind where. But playful, smiling Helena, a young German who spoke English with a thick Irish accent, was annoyed. She wanted to be near her Irish friend, Moira. They chose adjoining bunks for themselves, giggling like mischievous children about their rebellion.

I was in bed by nine, as on most Camino days. It was still light out, and I pressed my eyes closed, trying to ignore the sun's brightness. I did not realize that we were here on a national holiday until I heard outside revelry, excited voices echoing in street canyons below. It sounded like a party. Part of me wanted to be in on the fun, frolicking with foreigners.

And suddenly I was back in my childhood.

I loved summer holidays as a child but resented our family's strict evening regimen that included a bedtime far earlier than that of my playmates. When I tried to sleep, I contended not only with late daylight filtering through venetian blind slats, but also with envying neighbors. I heard them out there, recognizing voices, excited shouts and happy squeals of hide-and-seek, tag, baseball: "Home free!" and "You're it!" I wanted to be "it." Ricky and Johnny—Dutch kids whose family acted "Canadian," my parents said, maybe because they belonged to the more liberal Reformed Church—rode down the street with empty cigarette boxes clothespinned to their bikes, the cardboard rattling in the spokes and sounding like engines.

Back then, I already wanted to frolic with foreigners.

"Canadian children," my parents told me, were "spoiled," did not have proper supervision, went to bed too late. No matter that it was summer vacation. So, night after night, just as in Spain decades later, I waited for slumber, squeezing eyelids against the dusk, wishing I could close my ears to joyful aliens whose life included far more playtime than mine.

——

In many ways, we were marked—apart. *The Wizard of Oz* played annually on TV, late in the autumn. Margaret and I watched the beginning but were never permitted to see it until the end, since that would be after our bedtime. Year after year, just as the Wicked Witch started using her crystal ball to spy on Dorothy—marvellous name for a hero!—and her companions who were fighting sleep in the poppy field, my parents sent us to bed.

We were different, I constantly heard. *Better.* My folks had *chosen* Canada but also complained about Canadian culture and Canadian ways.

Those with British, Scottish, Irish names or accents were especially Canadian. They held headline-dominating power as politicians, union leaders, civil servants. Such people ran things and at times, disparaged immigrants, derided our accents, even telling us, "Go back to where you came from." So many things set us apart from them. It never occurred to us to tell them to go back to where they—or their ancestors—came from.

But we did reject them, look down on them—in our minds at least.

Canadian pancakes were too thick. As opposed to light Dutch *pannekoeken*, which were crepes really. Canadian gravy had too much flour.

More importantly, unlike our Canadian neighbors, we did not spend money on Sunday. We did not swim, go to the beach, or wear swimsuits that day, as did the surrounding heathens. We prayed a blessing *before* and thanks *after* each meal, more devoted than others, even those who also called themselves Christians but prayed only before eating. Dutch children never asked to be excused from the table. We waited for the final prayer before we could budge.

"Spoiled" Canadian children frivolously received new clothes each school year. We made do with hand-me-downs. Canadian children received expensive Christmas toys and wastefully got Easter gifts. We did not expect abundance or lavishness. Our thrifty parents had lived through the Depression, wartime occupation and deprivation, the stripping down of immigration—coming with few possessions and often without English, accepting jobs too menial for Canadians, knowing others would always have power over them.

We children were expected to be grateful, to have learned from immigration and the war. We were not allowed to call ourselves "hungry," even when a meal was delayed, when stomachs growled, when we felt faint from our guts' yearning emptiness. Adults told us, "You don't know what hunger is. Don't use that word. People in the war were hungry. Not you."

They lectured us about the surrounding culture's inferiorities. Canadian men went to pubs, neglecting families and paying too much for alcohol (it was cheaper at the store and more proper to drink at home). Canadians gambled, men on horses and women at bingo. Canadians did not save money, loathed hard work, formed labor unions. They were untrustworthy.

The first Canadian my dad hired, Mr. Goldfinch, had a small yellow bird emblazoned on his forearm. I had never seen a tattoo before. "He's been in prison," my mother told me as I stood by the dining room window and watched him load *kists* of glass from our garage onto my dad's International pickup truck. A few years later, our one-legged Dutch bookkeeper retired. My father hired a Canadian for the job, who then stole the financial records of the business and demanded a ransom for them.

＝＝

During the war, Dutch people rooted out intruders and spies by demanding that strangers pronounce the name of a Dutch city, *Scheviningen*, the Dutch "ch" impossible for many tongues. Similarly, our family sifted and shibbolethed what we knew of other immigrants, considering whether they had drifted too far from our roots. Our family gauged how Canadian other immigrants were, judging their degree of acculturation.

We spoke Dutch and disdained families who did not teach the mother tongue to children. My parents commended me because when relatives came from Holland, I could converse in Dutch, my first language—"free," as it had taken no effort to learn.

Another marker of our degree of "Dutchness" was that Margaret and I never said "Uncle" or "Aunt," always *Oom* and *Tante*, even to my parents' friends, even those not related by blood. Ironically my actual *Ooms* and *Tantes*, my mother's brothers and their spouses, preferred "uncle" and "aunt." But then they were more Canadian than we were.

⟫⟪

Yet we were also grateful new Canadians. Immigration is an ambiguous loss, marked by ambivalence.*

When my parents attended their citizenship ceremony in 1967, Canada's Centennial Year, they wore their Sunday best. My father took off a few hours from work, something he had not done since November 22, 1963, upset then by John F. Kennedy's assassination. Until the end of his life, he proudly wore the red maple leaf lapel pin he received when granted citizenship.

Yet for years he also continued longing to return to the Netherlands. Later in life he could afford to visit twice a year to see family and army buddies, but he found the country's political and social culture repressive. He despised its socialism and how everyone in a small country seemed to know each other's business and to have opinions about it. It took decades, but he gradually realized that he preferred more laissez-faire Canada.

As a child, I harbored hopes of visiting Holland, where friendly relatives handed out sweets and guilders. I had a frequent nightmare back then. I was in our narrow, pink-tiled Port Weller bathroom where one had to squeeze between white porcelain, tub and sink, to the toilet at the far end. The latter was always cold, damp, clammy. In the dream I was trapped and the only way to "get to Holland" was to climb atop the toilet and through the small window above it. I reached for the glass but never made it. The

---

* Pauline Boss, *Ambiguous Loss: Learning to Live with Unresolved Grief* (Cambridge, MA: Harvard University Press, 1999), 34, 58.

dream always ended with my eyes opening and my heart accelerating, blocked by that small pane.

⇉⇇

Ambivalence, or something worse, moved in two directions.

When I was eight, my parents rented a small cottage several hours north. My father allowed himself—more accurately, my mother insisted on —a week's vacation a year. The cottage was built of varnished pine boards. Walls did not reach the ceiling; they were more in the order of partitions, high enough that you could not see into other rooms without climbing on a dresser, but one could still hear what happened in nearby beds. There I first noticed the enticing morning aroma of bacon frying and how that made my stomach gnaw at itself, a feeling I was not allowed to call "hunger."

That same summer I endured carbuncles, painful boils on my thighs, to my eye looking like small volcanoes. They persisted with foul eruptions. My mother changed my bandages every day.

My father and I fished from a rowboat with an outboard motor. I admired his skill at steering the small vessel. Even now, gasoline fumes near water always smell to me of vacation and, even more, remind me of my dad.

On one of our first days I walked toward the noise of children and discovered boys—some my age, some a few years older, all brothers it turned out—playing ball at a corner where two dirt roads intersected. I approached and stood still, looking and longing in their direction.

A fellow about my size broke from the group, reaching out a hand to shake, a strangely mature gesture for a child. "Hello, my name is James. Not Jamie. Not Jim. And not Jimmy. James. Two disciples of Jesus were named James and a book in the Bible too. Kings were named James: James of Scotland and King James of the King James Version. Presidents named James included James Monroe, James Polk, James Madison. Famous characters with the name are Jesse James and James Bond. And actors, James Stewart and James Mason." I did not recognize most of his references and had never heard anything like this speech. It never occurred to me to recount the legacy of "Arthur." Years later, in high school, entering regional debate competitions and jousting with private school youths, I realized in retrospect that James's sophisticated speech was upper-class banter, coming from a world I could hardly imagine: the Canadian establishment.

Happily these boys included me the next few days. As well as ball, we played hide-and-seek, cowboys-and-Indians, cops-and-robbers. We had room to run, explore, and hike. We had trees to climb and fences to overcome. This was my first exposure to the starkly striking precambrian geology that covers much of Canada—we call it the Canadian Shield. I have been smitten by such landscapes ever since. The glass glint of water in the sun, hard-scrabble wind-bitten white pines, scattered granite outcroppings, and round elongated boulders that loom and lurch like leviathans from lake and soil.

When we wanted to eat or drink something cool, we went through a gate marked "Private Road" and trudged west up a dusty dirt drive. Never having passed such a sign before, I felt the privilege. And here was the next surprise. Our family had rented a small cottage for a week, but their family owned a house, a second home, with proper furniture and interior walls that ran right to the ceiling. Going to the kitchen to ask for our snack, I saw for the first time an actual Dutch door! Inside, the cottage had crystal-handled French doors, beveled glass panes with etchings of moose and windblown pine trees. I gawked at stained-glass windows, polished antique cupboards and tables. Everything shone and sparkled. The place smelled cleanly of lemons. Sliding patio doors led out to a porch that overlooked the front yard. Atop a narrow promontory, the house overlooked water on two sides and had a view of sunrises *and* sunsets.

The boys and their mother lived here all summer, year after year, the father visiting on weekends. My mother later explained that some people, better-off Canadians, *own* cottages. We immigrants could not imagine such extravagance, such luxury.

James's slender mother had medium length brown hair; she wore a white blouse and blue neatly pressed capris. Her made-up face reminded me of a doll. I thought her pretty, sort of. She played hostess, serving snacks and drinks. Mostly she ignored us and lounged on a cushioned chair in the sun, wearing oversized Jackie Kennedy sunglasses, reading, and occasionally tossing wry comments as we played and teased on the lawn.

One day, the boys and I rollicked near the porch. Energy was high and escalating. We shouted and laughed, pushing and chasing. One brother, playfully I thought, but perhaps he was annoyed about something, spat at me. Without hesitation I spat back.

At this moment their mother stepped through the patio door, in her hands a tray with glasses of lemonade. Seeing me spit, anger tightened her face. She put down the tray on a nearby table and lifted one arm. She pointed a trembling hand, red-lacquered nails on display, toward the driveway and said, "Go away. Do not come back."

"But—," I began, wanting to say that someone else started it. To say sorry. That it would not happen again. That I enjoyed playing here. That I did not want to give up all that fun. I wanted to plead against banishment.

"No arguments," she said. "Just go. Do not come back. Ever." Her arm aloft, like a cherubim with a flaming sword, directing me past the "Private" sign to the east.

How could things change this quickly? And with such finality?

Stunned by this sudden turn, I shuffled away. The boys said nothing, no one defending me or pleading my case. No one admitted to "starting it." Or called good-bye. I, and I alone, was expelled. I kept hoping to hear something from them in the next few days, maybe get another chance, but there was no follow-up.

At the cottage, tears streaked my cheeks, but my parents did not offer to intercede. Immigrants with accents could not make a difference with affluent Canadians. They shrugged, inviting resignation. I would have to find other ways to occupy myself. Whenever we drove past their private drive, I averted my eyes. I never saw James and the others again, although I later wondered whether I would meet him at regional and provincial debating tournaments.

I had no warning about their mother's displeasure. Perhaps she was unhappy all along about my presence: ragamuffin immigrant kid in hand-me-downs, pus-stained bandages on his legs. Perhaps she resented the presence of rental cottages near her family's privileged compound. Perhaps she waited all along for an excuse to send me away.

I did not care about any of that. I just felt overwhelming sorrow about the exclusion, about how easily others exiled me from Eden.

SEVENTEEN

I loved spring, winter melting around us, water dripping, small streams building, ditches gurgling.

Boys brought glass marbles to school and competed, rolling them toward holes we'd hollowed out in the soggy ground with the heels of our boots or tossing them at a wall to see whose came closest, often playing for high stakes—winner claiming all the ventured marbles. On one of the best days of my school career, I'd forgotten to bring marbles to school, but borrowed two before the first bell in the morning and went home with my pockets filled with dozens of glass orbs, clinking and clanking against my thighs.

Walking home from the bus, wearing clumsy buckled galoshes, as attractive as Frankenstein's footwear, I stomped crusty ice, watching it crack and listening to brittle shatters. I jumped onto glazed puddles, hoping to plunge through without wetting my socks. I waded in ditches, where runoff started to build. Calculating, always calculating. Watching how high the water line crept up my boots, not wanting chilliness to crest the upper edge. I hated soakers. But I still felt drawn to water, flowing or frozen, testing limits, defying possibilities.

The best spring game took place standing atop a driveway. I'd move to the edge to see the runoff flow below through a culvert. Then drop in leaves, twigs, discarded cans, wadded newspaper. I'd run to the other side of the drive, lean over, sometimes even lie on the gravel, to wait and watch for the item to appear, a small vessel braving dangerous currents. Even though spring water rushed, some items took a long while.

One day, I stopped at the Saus driveway at the end of our block and dropped a green bottle into the water, watching it bob into the culvert.

I waited and waited on the other side but never saw it. Was it stuck? Had it sunk in fluid, anchored in mud? Had it popped out before I spotted it? Did it float by just under the surface where I couldn't see?

I lay down on the gravel to look closer. Wondering whether I could angle far enough out and peer into the darkness under the drive, I scooted my torso forward. Still, my view remained too limited, nothing grew clearer. I wriggled a little more. Suddenly, without warning, my balance shifted and I tipped, head first, until my body swung over and I landed head over heels, prone in the flow.

I still did not see the bottle. But that was the most impressive soaker I ever had. I squelched home to change into dry clothes. It was almost time for my favorite TV show, *Passport to Adventure*, an opportunity to watch black-and-white vintage heroes swashbuckle—Robin Hood, Ali Baba, Jesse James, Harry Houdini.

The best immersions happened at beaches though.

One summer, my good friend Gerry's father loaded us into a station wagon—Gerry and his two brothers, plus two girls from our church, Alison and her older sister Janice. Alison was in the same grade as Gerry and I. That day ended in exhaustion, as beach days often did. I remember the pleasure, though, riding home at the end of the day in the back seat when Janice, a couple years older, let me lay my head in her lap. I felt soothed and still recall that solace over half a century later. Comforting bodily contact so rare in life.

Jones Beach was an easy walk from our Port Weller house, even in flip flops, draped in beach towels, toting unwieldy inner tubes. Neighborhood mothers took turns accompanying us. The summer I was eleven was our last in Port Weller, but we did not know that yet.

The Great Lakes were ugly with pollution, scum and dead fish suspended in sickeningly discolored water. We watched where we swam, trying to avoid plastic bags and floating crud. At home in the kitchen, my mother warned me not to swallow when I swam. "Keep your mouth closed," something she also often advised about my talkativeness. She filled a glass measuring beaker from the tap.

"See this? Guess how many germs are in that much Lake Ontario water."

I had no idea. She stated an outlandish figure in the tens of thousands. Message received.

One day my friends and I romped at that beach. We sailed on inner tubes, pushed each other off the dock, splashed in waves, dug furiously in sand. Just as I spotted a half-buried emerald green bottle, my mother appeared, announcing we'd soon go home. I decided on a last fling and picked up the bottle, intending to toss it into waves; but it slipped from my fingers and clunked against a rock. Not noticing its now broken neck, I retrieved it and gave it a fancy spin. It twisted, slicing diagonally through my right thumb's upper pad. I saw a deep perplexing paleness. Then spurting began. My mother wrapped a white beach towel around my thumb and hand. The cloth quickly grew soggy, stickily scarlet.

She showed no hesitation. "You have to go for stitches."

Fearing pain, I objected, "Aw, this will be OK."

But she had seen the wound's depth and knew better. During the twenty-minute drive to the emergency room, I felt light-headed, wondering whether I would faint.

A bleached line still diagonally disrupts my thumbprint. Later that year I read a boys' book about the FBI and the importance of fingerprint identification. Improbably, I had found a way to change one of mine.

Given my healing wound, not to mention Lake Ontario germs, beachgoing was over for that summer. I had no idea that I would never swim at Jones Beach again.

Looking back, I remember my exuberance in the moment that I swung my arm to cast that bottle. I should have known. Exuberance and spontaneity often turned out badly. I needed to be cautious.

EIGHTEEN

Recently, while working on this book, I wanted to drive from Toronto around the Lake and walk once more at Jones Beach. With pandemic restrictions, though, I was not allowed access. Only local residents—with proper identification—could visit. But were I permitted, I'd have gone searching for beach glass. I've always enjoyed such weathered refuse, turning it in my palm, holding it to the light.

Glass that ends up in water rolls and tumbles in waves and currents, over rocks and through sand, gradually breaking down and being shaped into smaller and smaller pieces. Saber-sharp edges wear away, smooth surfaces scoured. The glass takes on a frosty look, etched by sandy grit. It shapes haphazardly, though often into triangles or tears. Such trauma-induced transformations can take up to ten years or may go on for fifty; trash gradually changes from hazardous to harmless, even beautiful. It is rarer now than when I was a boy. People do not throw away jars and bottles as they once did, or dump broken windows or windshields in water; some abstain out of conscience, others because of stricter laws. Besides, plastic has replaced a lot of glass products.

Many people collect beach glass. Some for jewelry or art, others store it in jars or bowls, maybe in a sunny spot, hoping for fragments to glint in the light. These small wonders go by many names, including "lake glass," "beach jewels," "lake gems."

One of my favorite names—a little sentimental, perhaps too whimsical—is "mermaid's tears." I've been fascinated by mermaids ever since I was five and dreamed of one in our Port Weller house. The entire cellar filled with water, floor to ceiling. I swam and lived in the water without breathing. A buxom mermaid held me close. Green scales covered her tail and torso; her shape reminded me of my sister's Barbie. That happy memory lingered. For years I longed to encounter her again. But she never reappeared.

The other name I particularly like is "drift glass," something of worth emerging from a random process. English "drift" connotes meandering. Curiously, the Dutch word *driftig* can mean quick-tempered.

I loved drift glass even as a child. One could hold it, play with it, without fear of being cut—unlike glass I picked up on my dad's construction sites. Now I admire its hardiness, resilience, impressed that beauty emerges from discarded rubbish, natural recycling, a redemption.

Had coronavirus access restrictions been lifted sooner, had I gone to Jones Beach again, had I found green drift glass, I would have held it in my palm and pretended that the bottle I broke accidentally and casually threw fifty years ago, the one that sliced open my thumb and endangered others, was now transformed into a keepsake worth storing on a shelf, for marveling at and admiring, watching light play through it.

I want to believe that brokenness is not the entire story, not even the end of the story.

NINETEEN

Eventually a Port Weller neighbor—cranky and reclusive, who never returned our greetings, and who yelled at us boys when our bikes neared his driveway—complained about the zoning violations of my father's business, and my parents reluctantly began looking for a new property. "Too many rules and stupid laws in this country," my father fumed.

My folks found a few acres in St. Davids, liking the three-bedroom bungalow and a rabbit barn that would serve for a workshop. They agreed to a mortgage of $28,000, although they could not imagine ever having that much money.

We took our time moving. Most afternoons, January through March, Mom filled the car with boxes and drove them the ten miles to the new-to-us place. On moving day, the first Saturday of March break, my father rented large trucks to carry our furniture and appliances, his work crew loading and unloading everything.

That last day in Port Weller was unseasonably warm, and I played one more time on our half acre. I went to the back corner dirt pile where I had imagined so many scenarios over the years with my plastic toys: World War II soldiers battling, cowboys and Indians fighting over territory, pirates sailing oceans and scaling mountains to hide or find treasure.

A movement caught the corner of my eye. Looking more closely I spotted the last few inches of a garter snake's tail slide between rocks. It moved too quickly for me to decide whether I wanted to catch it. That's the last thing I remember in Port Weller.

The St. Davids place felt new. I had not considered the Port Weller house's half-century age until we moved to our red brick bungalow. Not many layers of paint on walls and no wallpaper. Nor lingering smell of canine feces and years of mold. No soot penetrated windows or smeared glass. No decades of accumulated dust and dog hair.

This bungalow was my age, eleven years old, and felt sturdier than the Port Weller house. Linoleum was not worn or cracked. All corners were sharply defined. This felt too good to be true, almost as nice as subdivision houses of relatives and friends. A new beginning for us. Unlike in Port Weller, I never tapped walls for secret panels. I didn't suspect hidden rooms.

Over breakfast one morning, sugary cereal as usual, I said to my mother: "I can't believe that we live in such a nice house. It's like a dream." And she agreed.

⇒⇐

On a sunny Saturday, shortly after our family's move, twelve years old, I went to my closet and retrieved a Black Magic Chocolates box. I had rigged it as a ship, outfitting it with a small hard plastic cannon, a prize once fished from a Cap'n Crunch cereal box, and then crayoned a skull-and-crossbones sail to mount on a short straw mast. For its unlikely crew I organized pairs of two-inch plastic figures: sword-bearing peg-legged pirates each with a parrot on his shoulder, spear-carrying Zulu warriors, headdressed Canadian Natives with daggers in hand, musket-armed American Revolutionary War infantry, British Grenadiers in tall bearskin hats, Icarus and Daedalus with unfurled wings ready to fly, all looking for adventure. Shaking red interlocking blocks from a tall canister's contents onto the bedroom floor, I built a one-story house with a secret: the back wall slid out easily. From inside, the crew spied enemies from afar and exited through the hidden panel, fleeing to their Black Magic boat.

I sailed them from my bedroom, down the carpeted hallway, an oceanic river bearing them east past the living room. Then through the kitchen, a continent of looming trees and massive mountains of kitchen chairs, table, and counter, where we stopped to forage for food and fight enemies. Then the boat thudded down steps, a mysterious mountain cascade, into the misty basement underworld.

Halfway down, I felt laundry room humidity. That night sheets would smell fresh and inviting. At the bottom, we sailed west. When we encountered feeble cigarette smoke ribbons drifting from my father's den, I reversed course.

≥≤

During the day my father's office felt tense.

His one hand gripped a glowing cigarette, the other a phone receiver into which he cursed. Bill, the foreman, often loomed in the doorway, hand-rolled cigarette dangling from his lips, swearing about Carl not showing up for work, again. Business manager John might squeeze by, lighting a cigarette before sorting invoices and checks. My handyman grandfather would push in, demanding petty cash, possibly for a new rake.

When I spoke, I often got no response from my father, his head bowed over a balance sheet.

≥≤

But I liked entering his office late in the evening, with no one around, to study his small library, a shelf of paperbacks propped up by two tarnished arch-shaped, brass bookends, featuring a depiction of Rodin's *The Thinker*. A Dutch translation of Hitler's *Mein Kampf* sat there, and volumes about D-Day, the Battle of Britain, and several volumes on the Holocaust and concentration camps. The latter transfixed me with pictures of corpses piled like logs and gaunt survivors in tattered clothes staring through barbed wire.

Once a middle-aged woman and her father—prospective customers— examined his assortment and she said, "So many war books. I wonder what a psychologist would make of that." My father did not respond; these folks might become clients and he knew not to give offense. But he angrily repeated her words many times in the succeeding years, adding: "Who's she? A psychiatrist? How dare she ask that?" On his behalf, I also felt offended by that memory. Her speculation, while not diplomatic, did raise an intriguing question. Maybe she'd touched a nerve.

He was obsessed by war. He lived through the Nazi occupation and shortly after that war ended, he volunteered to fight in Indonesia. For the rest of his life, he respected other Dutchmen who had also volunteered for that "police action." I saw him avidly watching news reports and film versions of the Vietnam War, no doubt reminding him of his own tropical battles, wading through rice paddies, creeping through bamboo, trying to battle elusive strangers (other culture, other religion, different appearance) who might at any moment kill you. Within a couple years, my father began to return annually to the Netherlands for reunions with his fellow veterans of the Indonesia campaign, reinforcing decades-old bonds.

My father watched the same war films over and over, whenever they came on TV. He enjoyed cinematic portrayals of D-Day, the Battle of Anzio, prisoner-of-war escapes. He admired those who played war heroes: gruff, terse, taciturn men who said little but did what needed to be done: Audie Murphy, John Wayne, Glenn Ford, James Garner, Charles Bronson, Telly Savalas, Arthur Kennedy, Lee Marvin. He loved accounts of the Battle of the Bulge and the surrounded American officer who defied a German demand for surrender with the words, "Aw, nuts."

<hr>

I heard a lot about "The War." On TV, even in a comedy series like *Hogan's Heroes*, and on cinema screens. In our car's back seat at a drive-in when I was six, I watched Steve McQueen run his motorcycle into a fence in *The Great Escape*.

None of this felt abstract. My parents had lived through the Nazi occupation with food rationing, the threat of arbitrary arrests, deaths and evacuations, listening to the Dutch queen's broadcasts on illegally hidden radios tuned to the BBC. My mom's close friend Tante Jos grew up in Indonesia, then a Dutch colony. During the war she and her stepmother were incarcerated by the Japanese in an internment camp. Rough treatment and poor food ended her stepmother's life there. Jos never watched war movies and resolved never to return to Indonesia.

I could not bear hearing spoken *Deutsch*, whether in films or walking through European delicatessens, although Dutch closely resembles it and I often understand its gist. From World War II movies I learned to loathe not just barked commands of *Raus*, *Schnell*, or *Achtung*, but the very sound of German itself—to my ear, it was all clunky gutturals and harsh imperatives, the very impression some have of my language, Dutch.

We Dutch immigrants employed a profanity for Germans, *Moffen*, a ruder version of "Huns" or "Krauts." We sneered, almost spat, our simplest, straightforward word for them, *Duitsers*. I found it hard then as a teen to understand my parents befriending a German immigrant who lived on our road, unconvinced when they explained she was "too young to have been a Nazi." My parents' turn for shock came when that neighbor's nephew visited from Germany, gave me an antler-handled dagger and lederhosen, and taught me to count in German and to sing "Deutschland, Deutschland Uber Alles," his national anthem. Later my parents explained that this was the song Hollanders heard on the lips of Nazi invaders.

A Dutch neighbor, Mr. Honsler, tall and grim, attended our church. I felt unsettled by his oddly sallow skin, the result of repeated bouts of malaria. As a Dutchman when the Japanese conquered Indonesia, he was enslaved to help build the Burma Railroad and told us that the working conditions were so brutal there that they buried a corpse under each cross tie.

In junior high I read World War II books, *Dambusters*, *Reach for the Sky*, and many volumes about the Holocaust.

I was born twelve years after that war. As a child, that seemed an immense historical distance. But now my math has changed. I hear about September 11 every week, almost every day. That was *only one day*, terrible as it was, over two decades ago. I regularly remember how my father beat and frightened me *five decades ago*. The war was not that long ago after all.

≡≡

The summer of 1969, our first year in St. Davids, my father let me keep his .22 rifle when I turned twelve. "Here, maybe you'll be a soldier someday, maybe even an officer. That would be honorable. It would make a man out of you."

Until then he stored that weapon in a cupboard in his basement office. I now lodged it in my bedroom closet. He also gave me a small cardboard box of .22 ammo. The carton's faint black text warned that bullets could travel as far as a mile. I knew not to shoot casually.

I don't know why my father had that rifle or where he acquired it. I never saw him use it. I liked carrying it around on our three-acre property though. The weight of its wooden stock and steel barrel convinced me that this was a real weapon. Able to hold only one bullet at a time, it was slow and unwieldy. Over the next few years, I fired it maybe six times in all, at clumps of mud, tree branches, stands of bushes, making sure that my target was below my head, so the bullet slanted downward, not likely to sail off and hit an unintended target a mile away.

I pretended to be a patrolling soldier. I frequently checked to make sure that there were no bullets loaded. I enjoyed cocking it, slipping the safety on and off, aiming at imaginary targets. It was my toy. I never had mishaps or caused mischief with it. (That came three years later when I received an air rifle; suddenly frogs and local shed windows were not safe.)

One Sunday afternoon, I wandered the weeds behind our house, unloaded rifle in hand. I knelt in tall grass, pretending to aim at Nazis. Behind bushes I wondered whether one shot could kill the marauding lion that I visualized. I marched stiffly, rifle against my shoulder.

Then I noticed visitors had arrived. Bored by fantasies, I went to greet them. My parents sat in the shady breezeway on plastic webbed lawn chairs entertaining my dad's cousin Art and his wife Annette, both in their mid-twenties, already married a couple years.

"Hi, Arthur!" Art greeted me. Annette smiled.

"Hi, Art, Annette. I didn't know you were coming."

"We decided to surprise your folks," Art said, looking at the rifle. "Hunting?"

"Nahhh, just walking around. No bullets. Playing war."

"If you want to be a soldier," my father said, "you need to learn guard duty, how to be a sentry. That's honorable, make a man out of you. Stand at attention, back straight, left arm down along your side, and right arm holding the rifle against your shoulder. Face ahead and don't move a muscle. Not your eyes, not your mouth. Nothing."

For twenty minutes I stood sentinel, fulfilling his idea of honor. I knew that he admired soldiers because of his books and the war movies he watched, and because when he brought our family to the Netherlands we visited military cemeteries, where he commented approvingly on the precise organization of graves in straight lines and diagonals. He stood at attention at entrances and saluted, even at graveyards full of deceased Nazis.

So I wanted to do a good job on this assignment and tried not to listen to the adult conversation. I didn't want to be tempted to join in laughter. I was not supposed to flinch or show emotions. I hoped to earn praise from him for my effort.

The group ignored me and finally, my shirt clammy from the humidity-induced sweat, I asked to be released.

⟫⟪

God, I want somebody to tell me, answer if you can!
Won't somebody tell me, just what is the soul of a man?
(Blind Willie Johnson, 1897–1945)

I didn't hear anyone asking about the soul of a *man* or questing for male spirituality as a child, teenager, or even young adult. If someone spoke of the "soul of a *man*," we'd assume they meant generically—as in the soul of a person. Back then "man"—as in "man-made"—included all humans, men or women. As we listened to emerging feminist insights, many learned to exercise more caution with language and realized that men had had a lot to say for a long, long time and needed to be more reticent. Others spoke of a growing "men's movement." Responses varied, including a best-selling satire that insisted *Real Men Don't Eat Quiche.*

I was not the only male confused and anxious about this. Growing up, men around me were not especially introspective. Most struggled long and hard just to survive—through the Depression, the Nazi occupation, fighting in wars, the penury of immigration. Their souls? They were happy to feed, house, and clothe bodies, their own and those of their families.

There were other challenges. I was bookish and introverted, a reflective dreamer. The hard-working entrepreneurial men I knew smoked, drank, and cursed. My father wanted to be a real man and hoped to prove that by trying to drink others under the table, but he always ended disappointed at how quickly he became drunk. Men spoke passionately of cars, hockey, fishing, earning big bucks. I suspected I was not a real man long before I ever even heard of "quiche."

Later, though, as an adult I kept bumping into "men's issues." An older man introduced me to Robert Bly's *Iron John*, but that did not compute. I wondered why we needed a *men's* movement. Hadn't the Crusades been a men's movement? And the Civil War and the Second World War and the Vietnam War? We men had bloody fingerprints all over. Did a men's movement mean that the privilege of old boys' networks in smoky back rooms migrated to the woods or Promise Keepers' stadiums?

Yet something niggled. As I grew more and more interested in spiritual practices, I wondered why women outnumbered men in churches where I served, at retreats I attended or led, and in courses on prayer that I taught—even in seminary.

In the middle of all this, a favorite singer, Bruce Cockburn, a Canadian, released an album where he explored the "soul of a man." I was not sure that he could tell me how to be a man. On that album he boasted of a fondness for guns, and I felt sad about his string of broken relationships. Some years later, I was astonished to see this social justice advocate endorse Canada's military mission in Afghanistan, even playing with a rocket launcher.

For years I thought he wrote the lyric quoted above. Eventually I learned that "What is the soul of a man?" is by the Reverend Blind Willie Johnson. Johnson blended blues and spirituals—two of my favorite musical genres—in Texas during the first half of the twentieth century. He was part street preacher and part busker. His was a hard life. He was blinded as a child, possibly during a violent fight between his parents. When he was in his forties, his house burned down. Homeless, he slept in the ashy remains until he caught pneumonia. He was denied hospital treatment—possibly because he was Black, perhaps because he was blind—and so died at the age of 48.

Reverend Johnson's "What is the soul of a man?" tells of a quest to answer this vital question. His singing voice is graveled and husky, and he's accompanied by a woman, probably his wife. He asks various people for an answer. He reports visiting countries to find out. He tells of speaking to doctors and lawyers but gets no satisfaction. Yet glimmers of light slowly emerge as he reads the Bible and ponders Jesus.

≡≡

Two times, two times only, my father took me, just me, to a film, a rare father-and-son excursion. I was fourteen and both were about war.

The first was *Lawrence of Arabia*. I was unsure, never asking, why he was interested in World War I. Lawrence was a tactical genius but his staring startling blue eyes conveyed madness, as did his delight in enemies slaughtered and blood spilled. After one battle, he looks drunk, stupefied, face smeared with crimson gore, like my cats after mangling songbirds. He unsettled me, not just his affinity for robes and obvious vanity. After the war, back in Britain, he was at loose ends—without purpose—and died in a motorcycle accident. We never discussed what my father got from this film or what he hoped I might take from it.

The second film, *Patton*, starring George C. Scott, begins with a massive American flag filling the screen of the old-fashioned St. Paul Street cinema. Patton marches up and salutes, standing as tall as four and a half Old Glory stripes. We close in on an eye and his saluting hand. I notice his pinky ring and recall that my father despised pinky rings on men. Our attention shifts to a ceremonial sash and chestful of medals, something my father would admire, and four stars on his helmet, gold braid across his chest, and ivory-handled revolver tucked into his belt. (Not "pearl-handled," because, as Patton says later in the film, "only a pimp in a Louisiana whorehouse carries pearl-handled revolvers.") He, like Lawrence, seemed ill-suited to be a civilian and also died in an accident after his war. Who was he?, I wondered. What did my father—a man who disdained to wash himself—make of yet another fastidiously finicky dresser?

Patton speechifies: "Now I want you to remember, that no bastard ever won a war by dying for his country. He won it by making the other poor dumb bastard die for his country." I had not heard such film profanity before, but my father enjoyed blunt talk and words not allowed at our dinner table. Patton added, "Americans love a winner and will not tolerate a loser"; "We're going to murder those Hun bastards by the bushel"; "When you put your hand into a bunch of goo, that moments before was your best friend's face, you'll know what to do." The audience laughed minutes later when Patton futilely emptied his revolver at attacking Nazi planes. Still, what to make of a four-star general who, according to the film, believed himself a reincarnation of an ancient warrior from two thousand years ago?

One scene still haunts me. Patton visits a tent filled with recuperating soldiers. A friendly father figure, he circulates, nods, smiles, asks people how they are. He calls one patient "son." He stops and ponders a heavily bandaged soldier, lying unconscious, then spontaneously pins a medal —a Purple Heart I imagine—on the soldier's pillow, bows his head in silence, appearing to pray. He knew how to look after his men. I recalled how several years earlier I lay in a hospital bed with rheumatic fever and felt cheered by visitors.

Patton comes to a fully clothed and helmeted soldier sitting by a bed and asks, "What's the matter with you?"

"I, I guess I just can't take it, sir," he stammers.

Patton pauses, and kneels, asking the man to repeat his symptom, who then says: "It's my nerves, sir. I just can't stand the shelling anymore." He holds back sobbing.

"Your nerves?" asks Patton, and adds, "Well, hell, you're just a god-damn coward." He slaps the man with gloves; the soldier cringes. "I won't have a yellow bastard sitting here crying, in front of these brave men who have been wounded in battle." The man weeps. Patton knocks the man's helmet off and yells at him to shut up. "I won't have sons-of-bitches who are afraid to fight stinking up this place of honor." He orders the man back to the front, threatening to use his revolver on him. All in the tent, medical staff, bandaged soldiers, other officers, look on in silence. I would soon know again what it was like to be struck and cursed by a powerful bully—and to have others stand by and watch.

My father liked that tent scene. He felt frustrated by politicians or intellectuals who mollycoddled "bellyachers," people who downplayed the necessity of war and violence or overstated suffering, their own or anyone else's.

We rode home in silence. I pondered his admiration of can-do, violent men.

Perhaps he wanted to be one.

Perhaps he wanted me to be one.

TWENTY

Within a mile of our St. Davids home lived a dozen Dutch households, with names like Poot, Den Bak, Abma, Veenendal. Our family pronounced them the Dutch way, "pote," "den-buk," "up-ma," "vane-en-dahl," rather than "poot," "den back," "ab-mah," or "veen-en-dal," even when those families preferred Canadian pronunciation. One family in town sold Dutch delicacies from a back room of their house, across the street from the junior high. My friends and I especially longed to purchase *droppies*, salted black licorice.

In May 1970, Dutch residents of St. Davids gathered to celebrate the twenty-fifth anniversary of the Canadian liberation of the Netherlands. We marched half a mile from the junior high parking lot, carrying banners reading "Thank you, Canada!" to the Lions Club grounds on the other side of town, where we listened to a speech by my future high school teacher, Henk Stokreef, a Dutch veteran. Schoolmates who happened to be riding by jeered out their car windows, adolescents often so quick to mock enthusiasm or any group that is a little different. I felt proud, though, of our appropriate gratitude for Canadian soldiers freeing us from the Nazis and staying after the war to help rebuild the country. Seven thousand Canadian war casualties were buried in the Netherlands, and local Dutch elementary school children still take responsibility for maintaining their graves. No wonder we chose Canada.

⇒⇐

Yet my mother objected to how others caricatured us, especially with derogatory English expressions. "In Dutch" meant being in trouble. "Dutch courage," unhealthy reliance on alcohol. "Dutch uncles" offered inadequate support. "Dutch treat" implied stinginess. Only a few terms felt neutral, like "double Dutch" skipping.

When I was a teen, she phoned the high school principal, a Canadian veteran of the Netherlands liberation as it happens, to ask permission for me to accompany the family on a trip overseas for two weeks in February. She responded angrily when he pedantically corrected her for saying "Holland." Yes, the proper name is the Netherlands, *Nederland*, but the Dutch often say "Holland" (two of its provinces are North Holland and South Holland). Only we get to determine our vocabulary and stereotypes.

Yes, some of us wore wooden shoes, even in Canada. Yes, my mother and many Dutch women raised tulips. Yes, the Dutch managed water levels and ground grain with windmills. Yet we chafed at false narratives or clichés.

For example, the town threatened by a hole in a dike until a little boy plugged it with his finger—that never made sense. Dikes are not brick walls but embankments, often covered by vegetation, that hold back water. Sand dunes or concrete or mounded dirt and rocks. They may erode, break down, be overcome, or swept away by waves, but they do not spring isolated leaks, certainly not hazards that can be overcome with one tiny well-placed digit.

Hans Brinker, a Disney film replayed every year near Christmas, was another unfamiliar story. Each time it came on TV, I asked again, but my mother told me that she had never heard of it on the other side of the Atlantic. This was an American tale, not Dutch.

In grade two, I read *The Bobbsey Twins in Tulip Land*, trying to figure out how the Bobbseys absurdly managed to get suspended from windmill sails. They probably tripped over wooden shoes.

＞＜

We talked about how Canadians treated us. We were outraged when accent-free Canadians told us, "Go back to where you came from." How were Canadians whose ancestors came from Scotland, England, Ireland better than us? And why were our hard realities not acknowledged?

In Canada in the late 1940s immigrants had to live in housing provided by their sponsors—sometimes in chicken barns, uninsulated shacks, or rodent-infested hovels. After sailing from the Netherlands on a converted battleship, my mother's family was put on a train to St. Catharines, Ontario, where they were met by Mr. Prudhomme, the sponsoring farmer who would employ and house them. Prudhomme, who spoke no Dutch (and my mother's family almost no English) drove them in his truck, on Highway 8 to Beamsville, delivering them to an old, dirty horse barn beside Lake Ontario.

It was furnished with bare and stained mattresses lying on the floor in two rooms upstairs. Their one *kist* of possessions—the only thing they were allowed to bring out of the country (up to 2,500 pounds was permitted)—took six weeks to arrive after them. Pieces of firewood propped up three corners of the one-legged stove. The other furniture items were chairs and a kitchen table.

There was no running water. Next door at another Prudhomme property, Oma pumped water for cooking and for cleaning the filthy barn. That neighbor complained she took too much and chained the pump. Oma wept then, not for the last time. Eventually a cistern was dug behind the house where the farmer dumped lake water; still not drinkable though, suitable only for cleaning.

Welcome to Canada.

≈

When my parents were in their fifties, they told me that their suburban next-door neighbors, Daniel and Aubrey, promised for years to have my folks over someday.

"But they never do," sighed my mom.

"Have you invited them to visit?" I asked.

"That doesn't matter," she said.

"I know why," my father piped in. "It's because we're not born here. We're not real Canadians. We've never been invited into a Canadian house."

But we discriminated too, dividing our world into Dutch and everyone else as Canadian, even lumping people with Italian ancestry into the Canadian category. They were different, definitely not Dutch, not among the truly chosen, the elite. To call something or someone Canadian was almost always a criticism, if not an insult.

I often heard, "We don't do that." Or, "That's Canadian." *Canadians* frivolously bought from passing ice cream trucks, purchased lunch at school or food at the cinema or on excursions. I was told those were needless and pricy indulgences, but they looked good to me.

Yet I still seek Dutch solace, sometimes unconsciously. In junior high, in high school, in university, I befriended males whose surnames I did not recognize, feeling a strong connection long before I realized they were Dutch. Two of them decades later, Kevin and Mike, are still among my closest confidants.

As a teen I tired at times of Dutchness, and eventually I would look for a church that was not so tied to ethnicity. But now I see the insecurity of newcomers in a strange land when many things changed quickly. Between disruptions of the Depression, war, occupation, and immigration, it was hard to know what was safe or where we belonged. We clung to reassuring cultural vestiges, as many immigrants almost inevitably do, while trying to understand others, a new language and foreign practices. Always wondering whether the losses and sacrifices of leaving the homeland would pay off, whether hard work would cover bills and mortgages, how things would turn out.

I chafed at our church's Dutchness and longed for diversity. I asked my parents whether I could date girls from other denominations or other cultures. "As long as they're not Catholic," they told me.

I began challenging our minister, raising questions, especially about the baffling implications of predestination. By the time I was eighteen, the *Dominee* would tell me, "You have a choice. You can attend young people's* and keep quiet or you must stop coming." This came as a release. I did not want to attend and so from then on did not. Within a few years I would do something that I knew no other teenager to do. I left my Dutch church community and joined another denomination.

At the time I marveled at how the minister's miscalculation freed me. Later, in my thirties, I wondered at his obtuseness. Now in my sixties I see him trying to hold a community together. I get that, even feeling sympathy for his misguided attempt.

* *Young people's* was an important way for Christian Reformed churches to retain the young as Dutch Calvinists and help them find ethnically preferable mates. They were not called youth groups, but always "young people's."

TWENTY-ONE

I still cannot fathom storing a dead man's clothes for years, a strange inheritance to my mind, let alone imposing them on a child, ordering him to don them. After my grandfather in Holland died, my grandmother sent us his pajamas and dress shoes. My mother dutifully set them aside for six years until I was twelve and had grown enough to fill them.

The clunky shoes did not bother me much or often. I endured them on my feet once a week. I polished them black and bright each Saturday and the next day clomped short distances from house to car and from car to church, thumping on sanctuary hardwood, putting up with their pinching stiffness through worship and then back home. They did not provoke my aggravation or resentment. But I hated the gray chain-gang striped pajamas whose thick fabric would never wear out. I couldn't wait to outgrow them. The flannel, warm enough for Opa's damp Dutch climate and our snowy Canadian winters, reminded me of photos of concentration camp garb. They had belonged to a dead man, maybe he even died in them, the last things he wore. If clothes could be haunted, surely these were. I loathed lying in them night after night.

"Do I have to?" I complained time and again.

My mother reprimanded me. "Be quiet. Stop fussing."

This astonishes my adult children. Why not refuse?, they want to know. Surely, they argue, I could have gone to bed naked or in underwear. I might have smuggled the clothes from the house, tossed them in the incinerator out back where I was in charge of burning household garbage a couple times a week, let them disappear. Any punishment might be worth it, they tell me. Why wear them at all? My children would not have obeyed. Perhaps we raised them well.

I never imagined such possibilities. Rebellion was always dangerous and futile.

≳⋲

"A typical teenager's room," she gushed, popping her head around my door.

My parents' friend Mrs. Droomweg was visiting them in the living room down the hall. We did not know her well, but on her way to the washroom, she looked in on me. She was just making conversation, just being friendly.

I said nothing.

I was in the mission style chair that my Opa Jelle had passed on to me. It had come over in the immigration *kist*. My mother remembered climbing onto it as a toddler in Friesland. Under the light of the floor lamp, I held *Oliver Twist*, a Scholastic edition.

I looked around to see what she might see.

Brightly colored pennants hung along the top of the pale blue walls, each proclaiming a different Dutch city that I had never visited or Dutch soccer teams that I had never watched. I was not interested in sports, and soccer from the Netherlands was not broadcast on this side of the ocean anyway. My immaculately made bed's dark blue spread precisely matched the curtains—all my mother's attention to details. A small antique secretary's desk, brought along from Port Weller, perched under the window. My closet door stood ajar, clothes neatly arranged.

A battered two-shelf pine bookcase held: a trilogy of Viking novels written for children; a swashbuckling account of Jews resisting Nazis, *Forged in Fury*; *Exodus* by Leon Uris; a sombre yellow and black paperback with *Jood* ("Jew") on the front cover, something purchased at the Anne Frank House in Amsterdam; *Jews, God, and History* by Max I. Dimont; *The Hiding Place* by Corrie Ten Boom; an elementary age appropriate biography of Johnny Cash (another Scholastic edition); *Tell It Like It Is: How Not to Be a Witless Witness* by Fritz Ridenour; several Tarzan volumes; and eight blue-spined Hardy Boys.

I was unsure what politeness required. I had not invited her commentary on my surroundings, not initiated conversation. I did not know how to ask an adult, "What do you mean?" Smiling uncertainly, I stayed quiet, waiting for her to move on. So much she could not see.

The open closet door blocked her view of my Age of Aquarius-era parchment poster:

> I do my thing and you do yours.
> I am not in this world to live up to your expectations,
> And you are not in this world to live up to mine.
> You are you, and I am I,
> and if by chance we find each other,
> it's beautiful.

One-eyed General Moshe Dayan, hero of the Six Day War, grinned from the back of my bedroom door.

I often struggled at that creaky desk, its tarnished brass handles rattling every time I moved my pen. I spent hours there, not only doing homework and studying, but staring out the window at acres of weeds next door and trying to figure out how to become a writer. There I wrote a novel at age twelve, entitling it *The Mystery of the Eerie Tattoo*. A few years later that is where I studied *Writer's Digest*, my first subscription to anything.

In Opa's chair, I memorized the Heidelberg Catechism, my initial exposure to disciplined theology. My small King James was stashed nearby, beside it a six-inch ruler and red pen.

Every night I knelt beside my bed, my fervent altar, murmuring confessions about turbulent emotions and urging God for personal favors, for help on tests and exams. I asked for blessings on my family and friends and always concluded my prayer list with this verse: "If I forget thee, O Jerusalem, let my right hand forget her cunning. If I do not remember thee, let my tongue cleave to the roof of my mouth; if I prefer not Jerusalem above my chief joy."

Guilt and shame pooled within me daily because whenever I rose from prayers and lay myself down to sleep I could not stop fantasizing about girls' alluring curves.

That bed was not safe, even after I fell asleep. Some years later I awoke at 4:30 a.m. when ambulance attendants wheeled my ashen-faced father away on a gurney. I wondered whether he would survive his first heart attack.

The uninvited visitor did not know any of this.

Nor did she know that the most terrifying occurrence of my first fourteen years happened a few steps away from where she stood. Nor that my most exhilarating experience occurred a few steps in another direction. Two events that still preoccupy me a half century later.

≡≡

The family assumed, and I did too, that I would join my father's business. He did not follow in his dad's footsteps—managing an agricultural supply business—but nevertheless expected my devoted imitation. When he and I saw "Paul Boers Greenhouse Construction" painted on his trucks or in green plastic letters on his workshop at the back of our property, he would lay a hand on my shoulder and say: "Someday that will read 'Paul Boers *and Son.*'" I nodded, never questioning my lifelong novitiate.

I observed and studied greenhouses, his domain. He was never interested in my reading or my school projects. So I learned the difference between North American models, heavily constructed with elaborately welded trusses to withstand snowpacks, and lighter Dutch forms that contend only with rainfall. Distinguishing hothouses built to last and those cobbled together. Knowing the virtues of glass—more sun!—versus double-sheeted plastic—40 percent fuel savings.

"After you graduate, Artur," his Dutch tongue never did pronounce my name correctly, "you'll join this business. I am doing all this for you."

When I was seven, I complained: "I want to work for you now. Who needs school?"

"The government—in its infinite wisdom—says you have to stay until you're sixteen. High school might be good. You could learn math and drafting, maybe accounting."

Back in Port Weller one Saturday morning, I stepped into his office, just off the dining room, and told him I was heading out to collect for my *TV Guide* route.

"What percent of profits do you make, son?" He was seated at his desk, a customer in a straight chair a few feet away.

"Percent? What's that?"

"You need to understand that for business." The men looked at each other and chuckled.

I felt stupid.

≡≡

In grade six I got along well with my first male teacher, melodramatic Mr. Hoekstra, who attacked the piano with manic passion, sucking his beard into his mouth, longish hair flailing as he concentrated on rhythms and tunes. There I first heard the term "blues," electrified as he banged them out. From the back of the room, I watched his silhouette; his keyboard pounding resembled a classical composer or mad professor. During art class, he urged us to lie on the floor and then joined us, suit jacket, tie, and all. At home I talked about his hair, music, linoleum proneness. My mother explained, "He's an artist."

My father—in suit and tie that he donned after supper—went with my mother to the spring parent-teacher's conference, a few weeks after we moved to St. Davids. I did not worry. That year I received good grades for the first time, tied for second best in our class, no longer criticized for daydreaming and staring out the window.

They knew Mr. Hoekstra from church. He played the organ on Sundays and worked for my father in summers. That evening my parents mentioned the business plans and Hoekstra laughed, "Arthur will never be a businessman. He likes history. Math does not interest him."

My folks regarded him as "a little different," but liked this feisty Frisian's boisterous humor. They had an old-fashioned trust in authorities, including teachers. He was younger than they, but they listened. The next day, my mother told me over breakfast what Hoekstra said. She was always in charge of sensitive family conversations. (A few months later—I asked an awkward question at supper, "What does 'have to get married' mean?"— my father would deputize her to teach me about birds and bees.) As she recounted Hoekstra's words, I knew immediately that he was right. That's all it took to persuade me, to name a different calling. After that, I never considered joining my father's business. My life trajectory suddenly shifted.

Until then I dutifully assumed that I would be "*and* Son." But one contrary sentence, casually dropped by my teacher, opened possibilities for impractical, unhandy me—all thumbs, uninterested in commerce. I did not have to be a businessman or understand percentages. More importantly, I did not want to.

Not that his apocalyptic revelation settled my freedom. Its barely authoritative ballast became a persistent counterweight for me against coming storms. With no other sons, my father lost a dream and his anger erupted regularly for years; cursing often, leaving me fearful much of the time. At suppers he sneered at me with the insults that he also applied to TV pundits, ones he argued with as he watched the 6:30 and 11 p.m. news: "so-called intellectual," "semi-intellectual." The fiercer he became, the more sure I was that I could never join his company. I chafed under his resentment but never doubted that I was not cut out for business, certainly not business with him. That would be a bad idea for me, for us both, for surely he and I would grow to dislike each other even more if forced into ongoing proximity.

Now, an older father myself, I know about longing to have one's children close. Our offspring live thousands of miles away, in another country. In his awkard way my father wanted to be with me, his son, wanted his son with him. His reactivity drove me away, but his sadness makes sense now. Only after he died did I learn that, years earlier, every time I drove away back to university, he cried.

⇒⇐

Later that spring, the conservatory where Margaret and I took accordion lessons put on its annual recital in a rented church hall.

Our parents drove us. My sister and I lugged bulky instrument cases and set ourselves up with rickety music stands on stage. Chairs scraped noisily over hardwood as parents, grandparents, brothers and sisters of the young musicians got themselves in place.

My father stepped outside for a cigarette or two and I kept looking for his reappearance. When he returned, he stood at the back, leaning against a wall with other dads. Something about how the light that evening caught him. His full head of hair—still dark, not having changed much—suddenly looked entirely gray. He was forty-two; he too would grow old.

But always distant, unreachable.

⇒⇐

I learned early to be cautious, tentative, with him. As a young teen, influenced by *Daniel Boone* on TV and reading about pioneers and explorers and First Nations, I admired those who could walk silently through forests. I practiced stepping slowly, not wanting people to hear me move through the house. In the workshop, he often had no sense that I was near until I spoke a couple feet away. Was I trying to avoid provocations? To be invisible?

I think about my father often, even though—perhaps because—he was the parent I knew the least and even though he has been gone for three decades, almost half my life. I once heard someone claim that we are most affected by the parent who is the most distant.

><

The summer I was twelve my father insisted that I work for him, five ten-hour days a week.

Mostly I tended the Rube Goldberg cutting machine. I set up lengths of extruded aluminum to be sawn into two-inch pieces, units that would fasten wood bars to greenhouse gutters. I measured the aluminum, slid it into place, then set the machine in motion to saw back and forth. Occasionally, I had to oil a joint or replace the blade. Mostly I waited, five or more minutes each time. The screeching saw tone escalated just before the cut was complete. This job gave plenty of time to read while the machine hacked at metal. I sat on *kists* of glass with *Poppy Ott's Pedigreed Pickles* and Christian novels about young Danny Orlis. In the background, the radio repeated Johnny Cash's "A Boy Named Sue," "Spinning Wheel" by Blood, Sweat & Tears, and the Edwin Hawkins Singers' "Oh, Happy Day." I memorized a lot of lyrics.

At the end of August, my father paid me fifty dollars, my two cents for each piece cut.

><

I put in fifty-hour weeks for my dad the following summer too, this time on construction sites. I mostly did go-fer errands, earning $2.50 per day. I'd find tools, hammers, chisels, saws, wrenches for my father or his employees. I'd fetch cigarettes from his truck or their cars. In quiet moments, I played with kittens that lived in the barn.

A young fellow in his early twenties, Jaap, worked on the crew. I'd never met him before. His denim shorts were ragged, cut very high on his thighs, and his blond hair spikey. He spoke only Dutch. A recent immigrant, he'd arrived in Canada a month earlier.

A group of us sat outside on overturned putty cans for a coffee break. Eating cookies, drinking tea, coffee, and cold water. Most guys pulled cigarette packs from their pockets.

A kitten wandered by, looking for a handout. I petted him but offered no food, so he begged from the others. He stood on hind paws and leaned against Jaap's bare calf. Without hesitation, Jaap dropped his cookie into the mud and struck the kitten, cursing, "*Ga weg, je fieze neuker.*" My father's crew was a rough bunch who swore freely—forty to fifty years later the curses still spring easily to mind when I feel frustrated—but even they were startled by this vehemence, especially at a kitten. They would not tell me what the words meant. "Go away, you dirty" something I knew, but the last word eluded me. Eventually I learned. It means "fucker."

=≡=

With a hammer I clawed open *kists* of glass, then pried panes apart, before carrying them to my glazing father. That glass resisted separation, vacuumed together too tightly for fingernails to insert. I couldn't use metal, screwdriver or putty knife, because glass easily chipped and cracked. Nor could I wear gloves, the material too difficult to grip. Once I wrenched a pane free; I needed to remove blank newsprint padded between it and the next one. That paper often stuck because of moisture.

Tugging a recalcitrant piece, I slipped and a glass corner gashed an inch-long crescent on my hand, first an eerie white valley and almost immediately gushing crimson. Half a century later I study the ridge of scarring, for years angry red but now skin tone, and wonder why we did not get it stitched. The scar faded, but I still notice it, almost every time I see the back of my dominant hand.

TWENTY-TWO

One night an unusual noise woke me. Even when I was thirteen, my parents insisted I go to bed early, 8:30 p.m. at the latest. Long after falling asleep I awoke to thumping from my parents' room at the front of the house, across the hall from mine.

This was not the time when my father hurled an alarm clock at my mother and it embedded itself in the closet door, shattered crystal scattering to the floor. The next day an employee turned around the door, the damaged side facing into darkness. Employees often repaired my father's rage-inflicted damage—gathering smashed glass from where he tossed panes, mopping up after he kicked paint cans over concrete. No, the alarm clock came a few years later.

Fists pummeled the wall and his foot swung against the bedpost, I imagined. Worst of all was an angry cursing voice: "You lousy bitch. Why do you keep bugging me, goddamn it? I work hard. My business is stressful. I have no choice. What's wrong with you? I hate your complaining, complaining, always complaining! Leave me alone."

Mom murmured. I could not hear her words but her tone pleaded.

"Just leave me alone. What's wrong with you, goddamn Ganzevoort? I'm doing the best I can. Don't you understand?"

Again, she spoke quietly.

"Go to hell!"

This is the worst fight I ever overheard. At other times their voices rose. One or the other would be quietly surly for a few hours. My father angrily trashed things; we were almost accustomed to that. But I had never heard him swear at her, call her names. I wondered whether they might split up, until now an unimaginable possibility. Two years before at day camp, a week of city-sponsored park recreation, I met a child from a "broken home." He told us about his father returning early from work and hammering on the bedroom door where his mother was with another man. I was shocked. Until then I never knew couples who separated, let alone divorced.

Can my parents fix this? Quiet drops leaked onto the pillow. I knew that I would not talk about what happened with anyone, not with Margaret, not with friends, not with schoolmates. This must be kept secret.

Then a gentle tap on my door. My sister maybe? Did she overhear too? Not knowing what to do I did not respond and turned to the wall; I did not want to be available. The door creaked and my mother whispered, "Artur, are you awake?"

I said nothing. I did not want to talk, not with anyone, not about something that shameful, something that might endanger me. Better to stay quiet, maybe my father will calm down, not notice anyone else. I did not want him bursting in, his rage enveloping me.

"Are you awake, Artur?" she asked again, stepping over the hardwood. I still did not budge, but breathed slowly, deeply, hoping she would assume I was asleep.

She leaned over and nudged me: "Please wake up. I need to talk. I don't know what to do." She shook my shoulder. Finally, grudgingly, I moaned quietly and opened my eyes, pretending to waken.

"Did you hear him? Yelling? What he said? What he called me? His swearing?"

I said nothing. She continued. "It's hard these days. He's grumpy. He drinks so much at the Lions Club every Thursday. Always in a bad mood. Doesn't talk or want to do anything on weekends. He's too busy at work. I worry he'll have a heart attack. What will I do if he dies? Can you imagine?" The idea frightened me too.

She spoke at length. Cried some more. I listened, made soothing noises. What could I say about my father? How does a thirteen-year-old console his mother? About her husband?

That night I became her confidant. At the time her trust felt an honor.

The crisis passed. Other items were broken and voices were raised again, but never with such vehemence or that graphically nasty, at least not toward her, at least not within my hearing. More and more, over the next years, my mother quietly confided in me whenever she grew frustrated—with his moodiness, anger, drinking, long work hours. Sometimes she asked me to speak to him. Sometimes I initiated without invitation.

It took years of being a pastor—and making mistakes—to realize that intervening almost always goes awry. Taking on bullies usually means bullies react angrily and then claim victim status. The original victims often stand back and leave you on your own. Best to teach adults to work things out themselves.*

Over time my dad would know that she spoke to me about him. He would guard his eyes and not argue as I interceded on my mother's behalf in the years that followed. He would listen without comment or visible response. I would see no effect on his behavior. Except perhaps, I realize after his death, to put further distance between him and me. No doubt, his knowledge that she confided in me, on top of his frustration that I refused to go into his business, added fuel to his simmering rage, and increased my danger.

---

* *Bully intervention*: Dealing with difficult behavior became one of my pastoral specialties. Bullies often thrive in churches and "Christian" institutions. I even wrote a book entitled *Never Call Them Jerks: Healthy Responses to Difficult Behavior*. Friends tell me to write a sequel and call it *I Was Wrong: They Are Jerks After All*.

TWENTY-THREE

My father admitted that as a young man—still an employee and not yet an employer—he leaned socialist, but that changed when he went into business. Then he counted himself right wing: pro-capital punishment, anti-taxes, favoring the Americans in Vietnam, worried about communism's pervasive influences, despising naïve liberals and duped socialist politicians and their "double standards" (another frequent phrase of his). He ranted about welfare sapping people of ambition and initiative, and about misleading unemployment statistics, as there was plenty of work—especially on nearby farms—that people refused to do. He argued that colonization was good, especially when considering Indonesia's political and economic troubles after the Dutch departed.

Lamenting social disintegration, he noted that TV shows, like *All in the Family*, featured ridiculously flawed fathers, undermining traditional respect for authority. He regarded Archie Bunker's opinions as largely correct even though they were mocked on the show and by wider culture. My dad identified with "I-don't-get-no-respect" comedian Rodney Dangerfield. When employees played the radio on a worksite and The Band sang "The Night They Drove Old Dixie Down," he was angered by the line, "like my brother above me, who took a rebel's stand," and remained angry even after my mother explained this was about the American Civil War, not contemporary hippie rebellions or the generation gap.

After supper, in his basement office, he tuned to a Hamilton station where conservative curmudgeon Tom Cherington hosted a call-in show. Cherington had a deep voice and loud strident opinions, many overlapping with those of my father. Cherington and my father were angry about much.

Occasionally, Cherington perplexed me. He took evident delight in Xavier Hollander, a Dutch prostitute who discussed her career in *The Happy Hooker: My Own Story*. Upstairs, I listened to his shows as I did homework, glad that some people took the state of the world seriously. I marvelled that so few understood the importance of politics.

I asked my cousin as we sat in my St. Davids bedroom, "What do you think of Ted Kennedy and Chappaquidick?"

"I don't know anything about it," he said. A couple years later though in that same room he wanted to talk about how funny he found Chuck Berry's novelty song, "My Ding-a-Ling."

Why did people not have opinions about things that mattered?, I wondered.

One night Cherington hosted a conversation on, "What's the matter with youth today?"

Fourteen years old, I took a risk and phoned, thinking to impress Cherington and my father who would be listening downstairs. And—who knows—this might be a first step to recognition and fame.

After ten minutes, I was connected.

"Good evening," his bass booming, "what is wrong with our youth today?"

Here was my chance to shine, to be eloquent, to be insightful.

"Apathy."

"What do you mean?"

"Youth today just don't care about things that matter."

"OK. Well then, thanks for calling." And he disconnected.

He added to the radio audience: "Not much to say. Just a kid."

≥≤

Every other year my father bought a new truck, van, or pickup, for his small construction fleet. Then he called Mr. Schilder, another Dutch immigrant, to illustrate its doors and panels. The company name belonged there of course, Paul Boers Greenhouse Construction, along with the St. Davids address and phone number. But Mr. Schilder could add visuals, pictures of greenhouses, blue glass panes filled with stylized blotches of color, hinting at flowers. He taught high school to pay bills, but his true love was painting landscapes and still lifes.

In his forties, he had a slight build. His face freckled and earnest. He parted his straight thin brown hair in the middle, tucking the long strands behind his ears. When I commented to my mother that this was unusual for a grown-up, she had a simple explanation: "He's an artist."

My dad parked the new vehicle inside our workshop, the garage door lifted high to dispel paint fumes. Mr. Schilder brought his stool, palette, brushes, small cans of paint, and yardstick. He measured and faintly chalked lines of text, lettered in essential details, and finally—best of all— painted images of greenhouses and flowers. Each truck took him the better part of a day—slow, patient work.

One Saturday afternoon, I was fourteen at the time, I happened by and he struck up a conversation. He liked to talk while working, unlike most Dutch men that I knew. I pulled over an old straight-backed wooden chair and settled in. We began by discussing the weather but I soon found him also interested in politics. We spoke of Prime Minister Pierre Trudeau (both of us dismissed him as sneaky) and the Middle East (both of us worried about whether Israel could survive). He listened as I spoke. I liked having a grown-up's attention.

Then I said, "My father and I are both right-wingers. We have the same opinions."

"You don't have opinions."

This startled me. "What?"

"You're not old enough. You don't know what you think. You repeat your dad's ideas."

"But—."

"Give it a few years."

I broke off our conversation. "I have homework." I went back to the house and headed to my room, where I fumed, sprawled on my bed, still believing that it was obviously right for me to agree with my intelligent father.

⇒⇐

I wanted to admire Pa. For working hard and establishing a growing business. For commitment to supporting the family. For passion about politics and unique insights into the news. For knowledge about how communism works insidiously to undermine the West, Canada included.

But I struggled.

With his drinking, for one thing. He got visibly and stumblingly drunk at the golf club reception when my widower grandfather remarried. "It's not every day you go to your father-in-law's wedding," he slurred, glassy-eyed. He sat at the bar beside a local Canadian celebrity that Margaret and I recognized: Uncle Bobby, star of a Toronto children's television show. I no longer watched that but still was shocked to see two respected adults inebriated. My mother drove our family the forty-five miles home.

Occasionally our basement grew thick with alcoholic fumes as my mother, frustrated, dragged all the bottles in the house into a peach basket—whiskey, vodka, gin, vermouth, rum—and then carried it to the laundry tub, where she emptied each one. The cost of that discarded liquor astonished me; our parents so often admonished us to be careful with money.

My struggle also had to do with how he treated me. Never interested in my school projects, junior high essays on the Welland Canal, Rembrandt, Samuel Clemens. Anger on the rare occasions when my political observations differed from his. Refusal to pay me comparably to friends who also worked summer jobs for fathers. Disdain for my lack of interest in business.

In junior high, I read a novel series (the title eludes me now) about boys living in British public housing. Their mortal enemy drove a small van and chased and persecuted them, insulted them, made their lives miserable. The author noted that the driver practiced two of the most despicable things that men do: smoking cigarettes and picking his nose.

One Thursday my mother drove me after school to St. Catharines for my accordion lesson. I told her of these enjoyable novels. Unlike my father, she listened to me about what I read.

"They say something funny though, Mom."

She waited.

"There's a guy, a bad guy, who picks his nose and smokes cigarettes."

"Yes?"

"This book says that those are the two most disgusting things men do."

"So?"

"Well, Pa does them both. These two disgusting things. I think of him when I read that."

"Oh, Artur, it's just a book."

I watched him smoke, as he worked, watched TV, read magazines; or explore nasal cavities, sitting in the living room, studying the newspaper.

I remembered that villainous van driver and wondered what else my father had in common with him.

⇒⇐

The second and final time he beat me, I did not black out, or block out the experience.

Fourteen years old, my sister eleven, we ate Cap'n Crunch one spring morning in the kitchen. Normally, our mother was at breakfast but she was out running errands.

We began bickering. Who knows what about? I was convinced then that she "started it" and deserved my verbal feedback, as usual regarding myself as innocent. But I often did tease her interminably, poking and pushing her buttons. When we quarreled, my mother frequently reiterated, "You two drive me crazy, especially you, Artur."

"I'm telling Papa," Margaret said, pushing from the table, standing, and heading downstairs where he worked in his office, no doubt halfway through his day's first pack of Buckinghams, swearing about inadequate employees and clients behind in bills, tense about the long list of what he wanted to accomplish that day.

I heard a roar from below and then the thumping of angry feet hurtling up the wooden steps. My stomach knotted and my groin clenched. My father loomed into the kitchen, face twisted and arms flailing. Who knows what already occurred that day, what transpired in his business, what unresolvable or perennial frustrations his work had stirred. The annoying problem of me, however, could get immediate attention.

"Goddamn it!" he cursed, in Dutch. His mouth a black cavity. His forehead furrowed and his eyes steamed behind thick glass lenses. He clenched his fists to his sides. "Why do you keep making trouble? Why can't you leave your sister alone? What's wrong with you?"

"But—," I tried.

"Shut up, goddamn it, and don't talk back! I'm sick and tired of you."

"She started it," I interjected, my voice squeaking and high. "She's the one who—."

"Didn't I tell you not to talk back? What's the matter with you? Don't you have any respect?" He stepped closer.

"Papa," I quieted my tone, hoping to persuade, "will you please—."

134

He lunged at me where I sat on the kitchen chair. He struck first with his left fist, his dominant hand. The impact caught me above my right ear. The surprise stung as much as the blow. I instinctively ducked and slid off the chair. I stood, faced my father, turned my palms upward, reached out, and pled, "Please, Papa. I'm sorry."

"Shut up. You had your chance. Always bothering your sister. Getting on my nerves. Why do I put up with this bullshit? I am fed up." Then, ambidextrously, he swung with his right hand, I leaned away, dipping my head, but he clipped my left cheekbone. Unlike seven years and half my life ago, I remained conscious during his assault. Punches and slaps came steadily, alternating right and left. Salty tears fell. My nose ran.

"You're pathetic. Look at you. Now you cry? What a baby. What's wrong with you?" His blows accelerated.

I fell to my knees, unsure whether he knocked me down. I hoped this new position would give protection. I turned and crawled from the kitchen toward the green-carpeted hallway, twelve feet from my bedroom door. My father followed and his foot landed on the side of my buttocks, knocking me off course. "What's the matter, can't stand up and be a man? Mr. Big Shot? Always bugging his little sister? Driving your mother nuts?"

Margaret stood on the far side of the kitchen, saying nothing, watching. Glad to see me get my comeuppance? Horrified at tattling's consequences? Wanting to stay out of the way of his wrath? I never knew. She said nothing then and nothing afterwards. I cannot ask her now.

He kicked, this time in my ribs. "Be a man. What's wrong with you?"

I stopped crawling, rocking back onto my knees. I spread my hands, hoping to suggest submission, surrender. I stood slowly; he might calm down. Then I made a serious mistake.

I tried to smile.

"Oh, this is funny? You wise guy, smart-ass. Always quick with your mouth." He launched a new series of right and left fisted punches. I put my arms around my head, trying to deflect blows, but his fists landed below my ribs, sucking wind from my lungs. I panicked, unable to breathe, thinking I could die like this, right here, right now. I went down on my knees again, longing for the beating to stop, trying to draw in air. It was hard to track all the spots that hurt.

My father went back to the kitchen. He noticed the multi-colored glass fruit bowl, the one that sat on the coffee table in Martindale and Port

Weller, and now on our kitchen table in St. Davids, piled high with shiny McIntoshes. He roared: "Goddamn it. What's wrong with you?"

He lifted the bowl in both hands and smashed it onto the metal tabletop, pieces scattering across the surface and arcing angrily through the room. Margaret cringed.

Choosing an apple with his left hand he flung it. It struck me on the forehead. The next one banged my arm, the one I raised to protect myself. I went fetal, feeling one thump after another, hearing apples careen onto the floor and against the wall. Sweet stickiness spattered my glasses. He pitched left and right, with the ambidexterity forced on him in grade school decades earlier, when teachers beat his hands if he dared—or just forgot—and favored his left.

My father spat: "I hope that teaches you, goddamn it" and turned, back to work downstairs. I cried, alone. Margaret stayed at the far end of the kitchen. Then, without discussion, we began picking up smashed apples and glass shards, tipping them into the metal garbage pail with its foot-operated pedal.

After twenty minutes my mother arrived and looked at the mess, apple chunks and sparkling splinters across the table and floor, down the hall; she noted my stricken face, my glasses streaked with tears and apple pulp. "What happened?" she asked.

"Margaret and I were fighting. Papa got mad," I explained.

"Fighting again? What's wrong with you, Artur?" she asked. She filled a bucket with water and added lemon-scented dish detergent, found a rag, and began cleaning up mangled apples and glass fragments. "You two go, get ready for school right now."

"I liked that bowl, a wedding gift," she sighed. "We've had it all these years."

Margaret and I brushed our teeth, sharing the bathroom sink, neither of us speaking. In the mirror, I studied my disheveled hair, pink eyes, blotchy cheeks.

Margaret caught her bus at the end of the driveway. I walked the fifteen minutes to my junior high. Louise, her teeth in clunky braces, ever friendly, sat at the table next to me in grade eight homeroom.

"Are you OK?" she inquired, a gentle smile.

"Yeah."

"You look like you've been crying. Is something wrong?'"

"Oh," I paused, "the sun was in my eyes walking to school."

She asked nothing more.

That day, and for years afterward whenever I recalled it, the beating did not seem especially noteworthy. I'd been punished by my father. Once again.

Around that time, my mother and I rode in the family's gold Cutlass on a weekday afternoon as she drove me back from after-school catechism, where we reviewed the question, "What is your only comfort in life and death?" We exited the Queen Elizabeth Highway and circled around the off-ramp to Highway 8. As we passed the Husky service station with its massive Canadian flag, I tried out an idea that I recently read. "Some people say the dividing line between love and hate is thin." I thought about how hard he had hit me and our feelings for one another.

"That's ridiculous," she said.

TWENTY-FOUR

How do I reconcile all that I know and feel about my father? What to make of the men in my world?

My father showed up at parent-teacher meetings. He attended church. Joined the Lions Club. Owned a business, employed people. Was respectable. Unlike many other dads, he occasionally gave me rides. To accordion lessons, chess club at the Y, church youth events, catechism.

In high school, I contrasted him with other dads.

Daniel's father never brought his children anywhere, whether after-school extracurricular events or visits with friends.

If Keith, who lived on a rural road, wanted to get somewhere he had to bike, walk, hitchhike, or ask for a lift from some other kid whose parent would drive. Or just not go.

Dave watched the family car pull into their farm on late afternoons, the driver door swinging open, and his drunken father sprawl out onto the gravel.

Jim's dad never left the living room or held a job. He drank beer and watched TV, approvingly pontificating about the Social Credit Party's monetary policies, its promise of a guaranteed annual income and restoration of the death penalty. He never gave rides and never took his children on outings or vacations, only to Social Credit meetings. He never gave them cards or gifts for Christmas or birthdays.

Rick was active in our Inter-School Christian Fellowship. When he confessed to being gay, his Mennonite pastor tried several times to exorcise him. That failed, and most of us ISCFers stopped talking to Rick. Forty years later, at a high school reunion, I apologized. He said, "Arthur, my home life was so awful, my father so abusive. High school did not bother me. It was an escape. What you're sorry for didn't matter; I hardly noticed."

Maureen was a favorite friend. After high school we lived thousands of miles apart, occasionally exchanging letters. I noticed that she never sustained serious relationships with men; I wondered about that but never asked. I remembered how her father made her and her sister wear past-the-knee plaid skirts (which they promptly rolled shorter in the school washroom). And how that leery man glared out the back door window when I picked her up for a church event, high school activity, or bowling outing with friends. In middle age, I rewatched *Forrest Gump*, weighing the woes of Forrest's abused neighbor Jenny, her long blond hair reminding me of Maureen. I considered what I'd learned as a pastor and while studying counseling. Pieces fell into place. In our next conversation I hesitantly asked about my suspicion. "Yes," she told me, "my father abused me in every way imaginable."

Manny's reclusive father, Manfred Sr., was an Austrian immigrant proud of having served in the Nazi army, honoring Christian obligations to fight communism. Manny was not allowed to have friends visit, nor could he visit us. His dad never showed up at school events, no matter that Manny did well academically and won awards. Manny told us at school that his dad watched the Worldwide Church of God's TV show, *The World Tomorrow*, and insisted that his children conform to his strict fundamentalism. Manny argued that dinosaurs never existed and that fossils were created to test our faith, whether by Satan or God he never explained. Twenty years later, Manfred Sr., then in his mid-sixties, made local news for clubbing his wife to death with his cane and then hanging himself in the living room. I assume he had been violent with Manny, although we never talked about that. Nobody talked about such things.

≡≡

Angry fathers, stressed fathers, violent fathers, withdrawn fathers, uninvolved fathers, drinking fathers, dangerous fathers. For all his abuse, my father was never the most outrageous on that spectrum.

Besides, he was my dad. I was like many who suffer one form of abuse or another: my loved one seemed normal. He set the only standard I understood. I was glad that he was not as bad as many others. Surely, he could have been worse. But when I became a father myself, I resolved not to hit my children—and I did not. It was not until I was in my late fifties, though, that I finally began seriously to question his behavior.

≡≡

On some days, I see the times my father beat me as two outliers, two exceptional occasions. Our family glass was usually at least half full of goodness.

There are days when I see the beatings as the tip of an iceberg. Especially as I speak to relatives and realize that not so far away in my family tree there was worse abuse of every imaginable kind. On days like that I come close to despair, pondering overwhelming evil. Our family glass overflowing with destruction.

Today—who knows about tomorrow—I still ache about what my father did to me, but I give him a small measure of credit. He did not allow violence to prevail. Mostly.

≡≡

My father beat me twice in my life. Years separated the thrashings. He broke no bones, blackened no eyes. He dialed down the violence that he received from his own father. He could not count or remember all the times Opa assaulted him. And I was then able to dial it back more, never striking my children.

Still, I want to argue with him.

Both times he assaulted me, my father insisted he was protecting my sister, the first time I accidentally injured her and the second time when she complained about our breakfast table tiff. In both instances I claimed I had not done anything to justify such extreme punishment, perhaps not any punishment at all. He always laughed at my apparently absurd assertion.

≡≡

At university, I took a religious studies course with Sister Marie-Anne Quenneville, an Ursuline, the first nun I ever knew, and she gave us journaling assignments inspired by the psychotherapist Ira Progoff. Once, she had us write a list of ten "stepping-stones," key moments or turning points in our lives. I named my birth, leaving my family church as a teenager, getting (re)baptized as a young adult, my sister's death, and—astonishingly to me now—the day I lost a fountain pen. I also noted when a cousin, a savvier coin collector than I, fooled me into trading one of my valuable coins for an unexceptional one of his, a disillusioning betrayal that lingered. But my 1978 list said nothing about what my father did to me seven years earlier.

Now, over four decades later, I piece together a mosaic from all that he shattered.

TWENTY-FIVE

I still ended each evening by talking to God and reviewing my day and its dilemmas, concerns about grades, and then, more and more, girls. If God is real and thus the utmost priority, what better way to know him than to converse. My monologues trusted God to do *a lot* of listening. I assumed God's care and interest in the smallest details of my life.

I read a Bible chapter each day and drew blotchy crimson Stars of David beside passages that predicted Jews would return to their land, certain that they referred to the state formed in 1948. I doubly underscored Exodus 14:30: "Israel saw the Egyptians dead upon the sea shore," proving for me that God helped Israel, not just in ancient days but also in the Six Day War. I felt outrage when a teacher inquired in the margins of a school assignment: "Do you really believe God takes sides in wars?" Of course! What about Bible battles? World War II? The Cold War? God's priority was obvious. Bad guys lose.

I felt guilty reading the Song of Solomon but turned to it frequently, thinking of schoolmate Laura's wavy black locks, loose to her shoulders, and reciting, "Thy hair is a flock of goats." I marveled at, "Thy two breasts are like two young roes that are twins, which feed among the lilies," a verse that warmed my face and stirred my body. I pondered Proverbs' counsel, "Rejoice with the wife of thy youth" and, "Let her breasts satisfy thee at all times."

Sunday afternoons I lay on my bed, swallowing swaths of Scripture, trusting that diligence would lead to correct interpretations of each verse, interpretations that demanded obedience, the Bible a codebook that only a few of us most faithful cryptographers could solve. At church I scrutinized preachers' words. Listening to sermons, I wanted new discoveries and insights but was also on the lookout for errors, potential heresies. I took issue with ideas that did not accord with mine, ready to dismiss an entire sermon, even a preacher's character, if I disagreed about the interpretation of one verse. As a teenager, I often phoned the pastor an hour or two after services to dispute sermons. He—always a he—was patient. Now, having been a pastor myself, I am impressed by their forbearance but also frustrated by what a nuisance I could be. A self-righteous prig, truth be told, even if I meant well.

One day Reverend DeBolster preached a sermon against abortion but told us no Bible passage explicitly forbade it. In the nave afterwards, I said, "You're wrong. Look at Exodus 21 verse 22: 'When men strive together, and hurt a woman with child, so that there is a miscarriage, and yet no harm follows, the one who hurt shall be fined.'" He thanked me for sharing my insight.

Another Sunday, I phoned Reverend Kuntz, wanting to argue. "Why do we have Good *Friday*, when Jesus was dead three days and three nights before being resurrected on Sunday? A *Plain Truth* article—."

"You shouldn't read that," he told me. "That Worldwide Church of God is a cult!"

"I learn a lot from it. The article shows that Jesus actually died on a Thursday."

"Artur." He had a thick accent. "I don't want to think about this now. Let me get back to you." He never did, not on that issue.

I see now not only my self-righteousness, but fear. A doctrinal misstep or scriptural misinterpretation might condemn me eternally, might end up with me being sentenced to hell. If Dutch Calvinists taught me one thing, it was that thinking and theology had to be absolutely precise and correct.

I do not miss such haunting anxieties.

——

When I began attending a public school, I talked about God and what was right and wrong. Students nicknamed me "the Walking Bible." I felt proud, because I knew that faithful believers would always be persecuted.

Other students quietly spoke to me about Jesus though. I was interested that people could be good believers without being Christian Reformed.

I liked what I heard from pupils who were Anglican, Presbyterian, Mennonite. I mentioned this at catechism classes, but no other catechumens—all of them students at the Christian school—admitted to knowing anyone who was not Christian Reformed. I understood that they assumed that we were "chosen people"; no need to get acquainted with other Christians.

⸺

I talked to God throughout the day, directing silent nonstop commentary heavenward. I did not listen, pause for insights, discern, wait. Mostly, daily conversations with God were ongoing processing. I felt glad to entrust someone with my preoccupations.

I would head outside after supper, wading in waist-high weeds. This worked best when days were short and dark came early, November through March. Alone with God, enfolded by deepening shadows and emboldened by isolation. Both of us invisible to everyone else. I learned early that solitude was my way to encounter God. No wonder, I now realize, that I often seek out opportunities to be alone; it's possibly the same drive that took me to my canalside adventures years earlier.

When I was fifteen, my friend John, blond hair and crooked smile, taught me to "lay out fleece." Gideon queried God by looking for dew on a pelt, and we too could beg God for communication tricks. "If it's your will for me to ask Lillian out, then let three cars pass in the next five minutes." When the answer was not what I wanted or did not seem clear (did pickup trucks count?), I reset parameters. I never did date Lillian.

⸺

My parents insisted on church every week but griped about it. They resented the demand to attend twice a Sunday. We went once, in the morning, and then enjoyed *Wild Kingdom*, the *Wonderful World of Disney*, and *Ed Sullivan* in the evening.

They complained about pious hypocrites sitting near the front who cheated in business. About how they (because they went to church once not twice and because Margaret and I no longer attended Christian school) would never have positions of responsibility. Yet they did not actually want to be church leaders; they preferred the fringe of the congregation. They lamented dry sermons, telling me that "dogma" means boring doctrine, and noted that men in church with Trudeaumania bangs didn't understand that Trudeau was a dupe, a gateway for communism.

I figured we would leave that congregation someday, maybe change to the United Church on the other side of small-town St. Davids, a much shorter drive. Visiting occasionally, we enjoyed the change of pace in this little congregation; we never saw more than a couple dozen people there, all of them friendly. And no immigrants. We knew them though: some from the neighborhood, others from my dad's Lions Club, a few from my junior high, another who owned the local gas station.

Several of the prettiest girls from St. Davids Junior High attended too and I was glad. I watched them at school; their shapes caught my eye. Glad to talk with them here; they were popular at school and did not pay me much attention on weekdays. One was Emmylou. My ensuing crush on her lasted until grade nine. Another was Debbie, who frequently did not wear pants or a blouse, just a man's shirt and panty hose, her nyloned leg visible up to her hips. Martha, one of the curviest, leggiest females in the whole school, was in my homeroom. During an art class, she leaned over her desk and worked assiduously at drawing on a large sheet of newsprint. Her low-cut white-with-black-polka-dot dress advertised cleavage. We boys in the room nudged each other and looked longingly at what dangled and swayed in her dress. She, Debbie, and Emmylou started making regular appearances in my bedtime fantasies, after I prayed and while I waited to fall asleep.

＝＝

Another attraction of St. Davids United Church was its pastor, friendly Reverend Styles, bespectacled, scholarly, soft-spoken. He preached well, and our family discussed his sermons afterward, something that did not often happen after our Maranatha services. He explained practical implications, not much about elevated theological doctrines. His sermons conveyed not lofty ideas, but a love for Bible stories that we could enter and explore.

One hot Sunday, we fanned ourselves with bulletins, his voice quiet enough that we could hear through open windows the cicadas buzzing electrically outside in the cemetery. He went on a tangent. "If Jesus was ever in love with anyone, it was Mary of Bethany." He paused, letting this sink in. Afterwards we talked about how we'd never considered Jesus being in love. Years later, someone might blurt, "Remember when Reverend Styles said . . . ?" and we all did, able to complete the remarkable thought about Jesus and Mary. Styles became one of the people who inspired me to consider becoming a pastor.

One Sunday showing up at the United Church, we were surprised to see that they were going to have communion. As our church discouraged visitors from the Supper, my parents assumed they could not participate. They were surprised when Don Styles looked out over the gathered congregation of eighteen—we were the only visitors—and said, "Members from another church are welcome to the bread and the cup." During the drive home, my mother said to my father, "Wasn't that nice that they let us have communion?" He nodded.

><

Sunday services there were subdued and did not feel solemn the way our own church did. I don't recall hearing "worm" or "depravity." I was intrigued that not only Dutch people took God seriously. I began to understand that Christianity was not just about being in good standing with God—so we could get into heaven—but that it made a difference in how we live on earth and relate to other people.

In one sermon, Reverend Styles argued against a phrase from the best-selling book and popular film, *Love Story*: "Love means never having to say you're sorry." Love, he explained, includes contrition. I knew he was right. Perhaps this was the first time someone spoke of forgiveness in a way I could understand, something I might learn to do: "It's not forgetting. Not saying, 'It doesn't matter.' No, it's a release, letting go. Not holding something against people. Relinquishing resentments. Wishing them well. Being willing to pray for them." That's how I recall what he said over fifty years ago.

After the service, Reverend Styles shook my hand at the door.

"I liked your sermon," I said. "Thank you."

"If you would ever like to talk, give me a call." I had never had such an invitation from a minister before.

So I made an appointment and visited Styles at his parsonage in town. We sat on lawn chairs in his large leafy backyard and discussed faith, books, prayer. He loaned me an academic tome on ancient Israel, and for the first time I understood that there was history behind the Bible, though I hardly knew what to make of empires and unfamiliar kings, not to mention lists of ancient dates, too many to recall.

≡≡

Our family, though, never made the United Church our own. Those visits were little holidays from usual obligations. We mostly attended Maranatha, my parents complaining about it often.

I studied with Reverend Geleynse, and our class memorized the Heidelberg Catechism's fifty-two sections, each containing questions and answers. The volume's first assertion, about our "only comfort in life and death," was "That I belong—body and soul, in life and in death—not to myself but to my faithful Savior, Jesus Christ."

I noticed that I was one of the few students in the class eager to engage the materials. When Geleynse asked a question, I always raised my hand to answer, as I always did in school too, but now with extra fervor. Christian faith was growing more and more important to me. In the car afterward, I told my mom that other students didn't care.

"Maybe they're bored because they hear so much religion at school already," she said.

This made some sense. But if these matters were important—clearly they were; we'd end up in either heaven or hell—why did others not want to engage them?

≡≡

I never doubted that Geleynse, black horn-rims and square owlish face, was in touch with God and that he could help me be the same. But one Sunday he announced from the pulpit that he was accepting another call, moving to Grand Rapids. I thought, "You just took away my last reason for staying here." The unexpected idea surprised me. A moment I never forgot.

By exposing me to a different church, my parents had introduced me in a small way to ecumenical exploration. I could learn from other believers, other traditions. Faith formation would come less and less from Dutch Calvinist immersion and more and more from other influences, including my subjective prayer.

No one ever told me that one might encounter God directly. Aside from Bible stories, I never heard anyone make such a claim. I hardly knew what to think when it happened to me.

I see the three of us in that long ago St. Davids bedroom; I am at the bottom of a metaphorical stairway, a different kind of triptych than in my grandparents' Appelstraat living room. This later scene shifted suddenly from misery and grovelling to a euphoria that I would afterward often wish to recover, to experience again. But no other mystical encounter of mine ever matched this one.

It was Good Friday and I had paid close attention to the service. This was the same spring that my father beat me. But I did not think about that on that day. I struggled, rather, with how my sins killed Jesus, pondering how I had disappointed him over and over, daily going from conversing on my knees before bed to crawling on my mattress where I mulled shapely forms and winsome hair, tight sweaters and short skirts. I wanted to stop, to change, but night after night I repeated the pattern. And Jesus hung bruised and bloody for the sins of my body. He died just for me, just because of me.

That evening, kneeling, I thought over the day's grim worship. I determined that with God's help I would finally conquer temptations, obsessions, fantasies. I prayed, begging for help, rehearsing sins, confessing inability. I cried, pleaded, pounded my head on the mattress, for thirty, forty minutes. Spent, with nothing more to say, calm gradually overcame me—a warmness passed through my bones and chest, even though I was less than two dozen feet away from where my father had pelted me with apples.

Then my ceiling slid open, becoming a large horizontal window, my room a cold frame below. Hunkered on the floor, elbows jabbing into my mattress, face tipped upward, I saw, looking down from the attic, a pair of faces, each a yard wide, faces we Calvinists never portrayed but I recognized them anyway, Father and Son, peering down from the attic. Both long-haired and bearded, and, most importantly, smiling. They reassured me, let me know that I was in their good graces. I had nothing to prove; I was loved. I raised my right hand, stretched my fingers, touching nothing. But I saw them.

I sat back onto my heels. "Thank you," I whispered, and I waited, wanting the vision to stay. Gradually it faded and I was alone on the floor.

A year after that encounter, I sat again with Reverend Styles on his back lawn. Thinking he might understand, I described the vision. I had not discussed this with anyone until then, unlike my first mystical experience at age four, when I quietly told everyone in the living room after church. He listened quietly, did not laugh or offer comments, but did recommend more books. He thought I might like *The Late Great Planet Earth* with its clever chapter titles.

For years Styles was the only person I ever told.

TWENTY-SIX

The family occasionally talked about that second beating. No one questioned the madness of apple pelting, the twisted tantrums. No one challenged a parent's right to beat a child—with fists and feet—knocking that child down more than once, denouncing him with cursing, oaths, invectives. No one—not my father, not my mother, not my sister who triggered my father's intervention—ever expressed regret or acknowledged that perhaps this was hard or that this damaged me. Still is hard for me. Whenever I mentioned that day in the years to come, my mother repeated the same thing, "You were such a terrible pest, always fighting with your sister. I thought you would drive me crazy."

I tried again and again. "It wasn't my fault. I didn't start it." My father laughed each time. All this too another family joke.

Why did he laugh? At the absurd assertion? The irrelevance? My stubborn proclamation of innocence? He said, "You never did anything wrong, did you?" In truth, I was mostly a compliant goody-two-shoes. Perhaps that's what bothered him. He understood mischief, uproar, disruption, but could not comprehend my being so well-behaved.

My sister has been gone over forty years and my father three decades. My mother, now in her late eighties, is still perplexed by my father's explosive rages: "It seemed crazy. I didn't know what to do."

No one ever said the words I longed to hear once, from just one family member: "This should not have happened."

Sometimes parents get angry, sometimes they hit their children, sometimes they beat offspring. That's the way it is. Reality. Little ones get pummeled. If they did not deserve it in one particular moment, surely some other offense makes it warranted. It all balances out. That was the message I heard, one I both believed and chafed at.

≡≡

According to a song made famous by Johnny Cash when I was an adolescent—among the earliest albums I ever bought—at least one person was made into a man by his father naming him "Sue." Men's movement gurus such as Robert Bly and mythologists such as Joseph Campbell have noted the absence of rites of passage and initiation for males in our culture. Gone are the enforced ordeals—vision quests, abductions by village men, circumcisions or scarring or tattooing, getting stripped, going hungry, bloodletting (one's own or beasts'), wilderness survival, quests for spirit animals. Those were the days, apparently, when men knew how to turn boys into men.

I can't say I feel the loss. I did not want to join Calvinist Cadets, our church's version of Scouts; I did not want to hike in the woods, sleep in a tent, braid plastic, or, worst of all, wear a uniform. Besides, I always disliked groups; I preferred to be alone; no one hurts you when you are by yourself. In high school and university I resisted fraternities, fearing initiations and hazing. In my mid-thirties, shortly after my father's death, feeling the absence of meaningful friendships, isolated in my work as a pastor, I went to a therapist. He tried to persuade me to join his Men's movement group. He gave me a pamphlet and told me that we could go to a forest, howl around a campfire, and beat drums. But that sounded forced, fake, made-up. I did not make another appointment with him.

My father tried to make a man out of me. Tried to make me someone who would stop bugging his little sister, who could take risks and endure pain. Our junior high planned to hike two miles to Fireman's Park on a Friday afternoon before Christmas break, to toboggan on its steep snowy hills. My mother didn't want me to go, as a couple years before I had been hospitalized for rheumatic fever and she still worried about my health. But my father insisted that I not be sheltered. I went, gladly, grateful for his intervention.

Giving me a rifle, encouraging me to practice standing sentinel, taking me to *Lawrence* and *Patton*, and even beating me were his unconscious ways of initiating me into what he thought a man should be. This is my theory. He would not have articulated it that way, probably not even thought it. Rae, an older friend, talks about his quiet father, one of a number of brothers raised on a farm. At his father's funeral, an aunt remembered when each brother had received his final brutal beating, always somewhere around the age of fourteen. That timing is the same as what happened to me. Twentieth-century rites of passage for boys.

The formal initiations that Bly and Campbell eulogize were scheduled and predictable, occurring when males reached a certain age. They were managed by the community as a whole, or by designated representatives, men who were supervised by tradition and were also accountable. While actual rites might have been hidden, they were not a shameful *secret*. All of this contrasts with the unpredictable violence of a man losing his cool and beating his son in the privacy of home, family members colluding in silence.

———

In mid-June only weeks after he beat me, Father's Day approached, and I felt sentimental. Abuse victims often do.

I went to the drugstore and carefully chose a card, admiring its flowery poetry. Then I wrote a long letter about how much I respected him. For being successful in business. For strong convictions. For speaking out on unpopular topics. For a funny sense of humor and good taste in music. For political insights. A long letter, two sides of foolscap. Perhaps trying to ingratiate myself. Abuse victims do that too.

I presented this on Sunday at breakfast before church. "Thank you," he said, opening the card, quickly looking at its doggerel, but not unfolding the letter.

I waited all week, but he never acknowledged what I wrote. Was he embarrassed? Did he not know how to respond? He dealt with awkward inconvenient matters by delay and avoidance. When he and my mother went visiting, he never turned down offered goodies. But if cookie or cake did not appeal, or the portion was too large, he simply dumped contents behind a houseplant for the host to discover and deal with later, after he was gone.

———

Twenty years after that Father's Day, he died. My mother asked me to tend to his wallet and then to drive to his business office and clean out his desk.

The wallet was my first surprise, thick as it was with several thousand dollars. Why? My mother explained that all his adult life my dad was ashamed of once being a poor immigrant, dismissed by Canadians as a "DP." Not wanting ever to feel that way again, he carried a wad of cash, in spite of risks of loss or mugging, hoping to assuage his sense of inferiority. For similar reasons, later in life he bought a new car every year—Audis, BMWs, Mercedes, and once even a Jaguar (he felt guilty about that last one though—something he had longed to have for years—and returned it within twenty-four hours).

Then the desk. There were promotional pens with advertising, business cards and orphaned paper clips, not to mention stray staples. I studied items that I pulled from the drawers, placing many into a cardboard box. Behind filed folders, I found a copy of *The Happy Hooker* and the Father's Day card, the one I had carefully chosen. He even dated it: "20 Juni 1971." It must have meant something to him, I thought, keeping it all those years.

But I could not find the letter. For whatever reason, he lost or discarded my affectionate words. Were they too hard to read, especially when he remembered what he had done? Where did he dispose of it, the letter I labored over? And why did he keep the card?

⇒⇐

What went on in his head? He toggled between sullen silence and flaring rage. Much of the time he was depressed, I see now.

Many cultures discourage men from showing or discussing emotions. Only rage is allowed. It can be regarded as understandable, although not necessarily laudable. Anger then becomes a way for men to show agency. Many men I grew up with were rough, emotionally and often physically— ongoing jostling and competition, put-downs and one-upping. Never backing down, never saying sorry, never acknowledging their harm, never making repairs.

TWENTY-SEVEN

We occasionally found a way to play. He'd load the turntable and my head would bob instinctively, toes tap automatically, thighs and knees bounce reflexively, fingers snap unconsciously. He raised me on old-time jazz: New Orleans (where Louis Armstrong grew up), ragtime, boogie-woogie, honky-tonk, swing, and big bands, especially Glenn Miller and Benny Goodman. We knew what we liked but could not say why. Years later, the evangelizing efforts of my sophisticated jazz aficionado friends never budged me much beyond Dixieland.

To this day, bent notes or clarinet wails stir me to euphoria. If alone when jazz or blues move me—they often do—I dance exuberantly, Spirit-possessed, like the Pentecostals who worshiped next door to our church parking lot. I get up, wave arms, spin my body, moan and whistle, torso swaying and hips swiveling, feet sliding and shuffling over the floor. I scare the cat and come as close as I can to ecstasy. In the magic of music God touches me.

Neither my mother nor my sister understood. Swinging rhythms did not attract them. When they came home early from shopping, our house hummed and shook from my father's loud disk spinning. Appalled, they hurried into the house to turn down the volume. I'd grin.

He and I did not speak about the fine points of what we heard: cadence, cross-rhythm, polytonal, minor keys. We never discussed Armstrong's scat singing. I knew nothing of bebop or fusion or free jazz. As a former drummer, he probably understood downbeats and backbeats, but they never came up. Nor whether a band played "tight" or "swang." We liked something or didn't. No explanation needed and we always agreed.

My father grabbed pencils or knife and fork and tapped rhythms on pads of paper, tables, plates, pots and pans. At weddings or Lions Club dances, he asked bands if he could sit in briefly on drums. In his fifties, looking for a hobby, he bought a used drum kit to play in the basement.

A family visited us one Sunday and Pa put the Dutch Swing College Band on the stereo. The visiting father showed no interest.

"You can't learn to like this music," my dad said. "You either do or you don't."

Wiseass, fourteen-year-old me piped in: "Yeah, it's just natural. You hear the music, your body moves. It has to."

Our guest remained unconvinced. I did not care. My father and I got it. What more did I need?

≡≡

Yet he did not tolerate my musical exploration. I gradually expanded my tastes, not to supersede or eliminate love for jazz, but to include other genres. I explored country, especially folksy John Denver, Johnny Cash's rhythmic boom-chicka-boom, sultry Tanya Tucker. I listened to rockabilly, with its blues connections, and admired early rock and rollers Jerry Lee Lewis, Little Richard, and Chuck Berry. I went for docile rock too: Cat Stevens, Jim Croce, Linda Ronstadt, Olivia Newton-John. My father showed no interest. He didn't know, and would not care, that my tastes were tame. He disliked whatever "kids" listened to.

The Canadian group *Ocean* had a hit, "Put Your Hand in the Hand," and I loved the rhythm and religion of it, happily buying their album, another of my early LPs. Once, the family out for the evening, I studied in my bedroom, sitting at that squeaky desk, upping the volume as loud as my small speakers could manage. I didn't hear the family return. My father startled me by leaning into my room and yelling, "Turn off that garbage! That's no way to study." And I wondered why he—who loved to denounce "double standards"—could blare music but not I.

≡≡

That summer, I worked for him again.

One July evening, we headed home in his pickup truck, ladders strapped on its rack. Paint cans, toolboxes, and a wooden *kist* packed with drills and extension cords rattled in the back. We wore frayed, paint-and-putty-spattered short-sleeved shirts and long pants. Our battered steel-toed construction boots tracked mud from the site onto the floor of the cluttered cab, where coffee-stained Styrofoam cups tumbled around our feet. Empty Buckingham cigarette packages littered the dashboard and seat. Open windows let in dust and humid, stifling air. Work trucks had no air-conditioning.

We had put in a ten-hour day, not counting the hour-long drive to work early that morning. In the sun, we sweated nonstop and drank gallons of chilled fruit-flavored water. Arms ached from endless lifting and hammering. We looked forward to eating the supper my mom would have cooked, and to drinking cold beer. My parents allowed underage me, only fourteen, to drink alcohol at home. Dutch people didn't worry about drinking laws. After a construction day like that, a chilled Old Vienna felt welcome.

We said little and listened to the radio. My father enjoyed sentimental music: Roger Miller, James Last, Roger Whittaker, Herb Albert & the Tijuana Brass. I didn't mind it either (as if I had a choice). We both liked the station's conservative news presentation and right-wing editorials.

Not many six o'clock headlines caught our attention. But then this: "Legendary trumpeter Louis Armstrong died in his sleep of a heart attack. He would have been seventy next month."

My father and I loved Satchmo. We admired his trumpet deftness. We adored the showmanship and antics of this popular performer who appeared on TV variety shows hosted by Ed Sullivan, Flip Wilson, Johnny Cash, Dean Martin. We smiled at his broad toothy grin, his wide eyes opened comically, mopping his bald perspiration with a large white handkerchief, and the gravelly voice, especially when he ended songs with, "Ohhhh yeahhhhh!" Whenever particularly moved by jazz, not necessarily Louis Armstrong, one or both of us often imitated him by singing a fervent "Ohhhh yeahhhhh!"—our version of "Amen!" Listening to jazz was as close as we came to a shared religious experience.

My father took his eyes off the highway. Looking at each other, we gently shook our heads and said nothing. Years later, my father occasionally referred to that moment: "Remember when we were in the truck and heard about Louis Armstrong?" I always did and was always surprised that he recollected that sentimental moment too.

It was enough, just to acknowledge one other briefly and then carry on with private thoughts, each feeling our loss.

TWENTY-EIGHT

My parents pulling us from Calvin and sending us to public school had unforeseen consequences.

The boys who were my closest friends in previous years—Gary, Ludolph, Ernie—never came to our house anymore. Nor did I visit theirs or attend their birthday parties. There was no animosity; we simply lost contact.

When I attended catechism classes or young people's, others were friendly but we did not have much to talk about.

In high school, I made friends at Inter-School Christian Fellowship (ISCF), most of them Mennonite. Unlike my Christian Reformed friends, they liked to talk about Jesus, their Bible readings, what happened in daily devotions, and how to witness to our faith. I often ate lunch with other ISCFers who talked about "winning souls for Jesus" and about whom they hoped to convert, who was on their prayer list to become Christian. We reported excitedly about how God answered particular prayers. They challenged some of my ideas, arguing for example in favor of believer's baptism—that only those who professed faith in Jesus should be baptized. I studied our Heidelberg Catechism and talked about how the children of believers were accepted as part of a covenant. No one seemed convinced. I grew unsure too.

At catechism and young people's though, when I spoke about witnessing, others said: "We don't need to do that. God already predestined who goes to heaven or hell." I began to wonder why our church was only Dutch. Wasn't Jesus interested in other nationalities?

I felt more at home with the ISCFers and started visiting them in their homes.

⇒⇐

A good number of the ISCFers, particularly the ones most interesting to me, all went to the same local Mennonite church, the Chapel.*

The Chapel had an energetic youth program, a couple of dozen teens who did a lot of things together: attending Sunday night service and then hanging out at someone's house, Wednesday evening Bible study (often taught by the pastor), Friday night youth group for worship and sharing and fun activities (hayrides, costume parties), and sometimes more hanging out on Saturday evenings too.

I always felt welcome. I understood and appreciated their priorities. I could have fun. I laughed and let loose. I was easygoing and relaxed when I associated with them. I liked what they brought out in me.

⇒⇐

One Saturday in May, when I was in my early fifties, I was running errands so I could get our yard in shape for the summer, picking up supplies for working outside. I passed a church youth group holding a car wash fundraiser. Dressed in casual clothes, shorts and jeans, they all smiled. Buckets, rags, and hoses were scattered on the pavement. The ground was splashed wet. Vehicles glimmered in the light. It looked like fun, even for someone who seldom washes his own car.

Suddenly I was happy.

A day that shimmers for me from my adolescence was a Chapel youth fundraiser. At this point, changing denominations had not yet occurred to me; that crisis was to come the following year.

My good friends held a car wash to raise money to visit with Christian converts at Mennonite churches in Quebec. It was a beautiful day to be

* *Mennonites* are named after Menno Simons, a former priest in Friesland in the sixteenth century. A Mennonite historian once told me that everything we need to know about Menno can be understood by the fact that he was a Frisian peasant and therefore stubborn. Many Mennonites, like those at the Chapel, had long ago Dutch ancestry.

158

outside. And I had the time to spare. I was thinking about going on that trip too. So I joined them to help raise money.

The Chapel was located on an isolated country road, not the best spot to attract customers for fundraising. We worked instead in the nearest town, Virgil, where the local credit union allowed us to use its driveway and parking lot, not to mention its running water. The credit union's vice president was also a Chapel member.

The day was predictable, even clichéd. We eagerly counted cash as it mounted up, especially grateful for and excited by tips. Inevitably, boys chased girls with buckets of soapy water. Hoses were not always pointed at the cars. We all got wet. The water chilled and invigorated us but soon evaporated under the sun's direct heat. We laughed a lot.

I was rowdier and giddier than normal. I did more than my share of splashing and spraying. When a twenty-something man drove up in his Corvette, I took command. Without consultation, I decided that I needed to be the one to move the vehicle from station to station and that this chariot even needed a little extra driving around, some test turns. My friends let me get away with my obnoxious usurping. The young man looked amused. That evening, after supper, I eagerly phoned my girlfriend and told her in lavish detail about the adventure of the whole day.

What was the big deal? Why was I so excited? So happy? It was only a car wash. Why does that one day stand out decades later?

It was an exceptional moment in my adolescence. I was learning to let loose. I was relaxing. I saw that people could enjoy my company even when I was annoying—dowsing girls who claimed to be uninterested, hogging the hottest car from my buddies.

That was a different way for me to function. As a youth I was very, very serious. I thought a lot about always doing the right thing and being responsible. I wasted little time. I was intense and frequently argued and debated about the importance of ethics and responsibility. I wanted my theology exactly right and felt a missionary urge to straighten out everyone else's doctrine, mostly trying to get others to agree with me.

I was driven when it came to schoolwork. I wanted good grades. At age thirteen, I studied so hard and long for everything—even the simplest spelling tests, which I invariably aced—that I started sleepwalking because of stress. Part of me competed against others, always battling for first or second place and longing for trophies and being mentioned on honors lists.

Just as much I competed against myself; I always hoped to do better. Taking off a whole day from studies, just to wash cars, was no small thing.

=≡=

When I was eighteen, I had a dream. I sat in Maranatha on a Sunday. Reverend Kuntz preached about the superiority of Christian schools. Annoyed, I got up and by myself I walked out of the service, leaving my family behind. Kuntz pursued me and asked to talk. I felt too angry to converse but gradually calmed down. I told him that lots of good came from my attending a public school. I was pleased that he listened, but he could not persuade me to return to the service.

I continued to grow dissatisfied with young people's. To my mind, they spent too much time discussing opinions and not enough time studying the Bible. I noted their exuberance for having coffee and goodies, going bowling, and seeing movies—*The Three Musketeers*, or the pinko propaganda film *The Trial of Billy Jack*. Happily to my mind, as I already explained, soon I was banned from attending.

Further, I felt troubled that many in our congregation did not have the "assurance of salvation." Many did not dare to believe that they might go to heaven. This smacked of inadequate church teaching to me. Surely, everyone who believed in Jesus was saved. Why did the ministers not come out and say that?

Along with Mennonite friends, I often attended various evangelical events in the area: concerts, plays, films, rallies, and "crusades" to win new converts. I became a regular at a ministry called the "Lord's Barn," an outgrowth of the late sixties, early seventies Jesus movement—started by hippies who became Christians and then sought to minister to street people and disenchanted youths. It was charismatically influenced, not tied to any particular church, and involved lively music and exuberant worship.

At evangelical rallies and crusades I saw folks of many traditions—Mennonite, Baptist, Presbyterian, Pentecostal, Missionary Alliance—but seldom anyone from my own denomination. Like other Christian churches that evangelicals suspected—Roman Catholic, Orthodox—my own church was hardly ever represented. I began to believe being an evangelical Christian was more important than denominational membership. My evangelical friends and I often said, "I'm a Christian first and a member of

160

a denomination second." But we meant a certain kind of Christian: one comfortable with "born again" language, one who believed in and practiced evangelism. Influenced by Bill Bright's *Four Spiritual Laws*, we distinguished between "fleshly" (uncommitted) Christians and "spiritual" Christians who were certainly on the best road to heaven. Looking at my congregation, I dismissed many members as second-class Christians at best. Yes, I was arrogant and self-righteous.

≡≡

The winter I was eighteen, Chapel youth planned to go on a retreat in Muskoka. It was the same time as a regional debating tournament. I had won awards debating in the past but decided that I was tired of defeating others in arguments and would rather go away with beloved believers. I had already signed up for that Chapel retreat when Maranatha's young people's announced a retreat the same weekend. Without regret, I decided to stick with my original plan.

We drove several hours to a camp. The weekend was an adrenaline-fueled time of fun. Midwinter, the snow was deep and heaters and water pipes both failed. The weather was subzero (Fahrenheit) and we had to haul our gear a long way through drifts. The electricity was intermittent and weak. (We'd brought along tapes of Paul Little, a popular Christian speaker, but the feeble electrical outlet only drove the tape player at three-quarters speed, humorously altering his recorded voice.) We were not skilled at heating huts with wood, and at one point the pipe leading out of our wood stove glowed red hot. But everything was fun. It was all an adventure. We laughed frequently, singing songs and having snowball fights. Even the long ride home in a crowded van was enjoyable.

A few weeks after the retreat, a Mennonite friend—who had enjoyed the weekend as much as I did—expressed doubt about my choice: "I feel bad that you didn't go to your youth group's weekend." We were sitting at carrels in the high school library. That moment I began to ponder seriously a question I had not yet explicitly considered. Should I change churches?

Perhaps in retrospect the choice seems obvious, but it wasn't for me at that time. In the 1970s denominational ties and loyalties were still strong. I did not know anyone who changed from a denomination of their upbringing to another of their choice. "Church shopping" and "seeker churches" were concepts yet to be invented, let alone named. Add to that the strong ethnic ties of my Dutch Calvinist denomination, and it made changing churches more complicated.

I felt increasingly at home with the Mennonites and like an outsider at Maranatha. In the previous year, my name was put forward for nomination to be on the leadership of our young people's. Given my enthusiastic Christian faith, good grades at school, and position as president of the local ISCF, I might have seemed an obvious candidate. My nomination was turned down, without explanation. That still annoyed me, but by now I was not even allowed to attend anyway.

I mostly agreed with Christian Reformed beliefs, although questions about evangelism, predestination, and baptism niggled. I felt the theology was too abstract, too distant. Christian life could be summarized by John 1:12 (RSV): "To all who received him, who believed in his name, he gave power to become children of God." The essentials included three verbs: receive, believe, and become. Maranatha sermons only mentioned *believing* and did not explicitly encourage people to *receive* ("accept Jesus"), let alone explain how to be or *become* Christian. I knew that if I had a non-Christian friend, I would not bring them to Maranatha: they would feel excluded by not being Dutch and would not hear a clear statement of the gospel.

But I did not know anyone who had left Maranatha for another denomination, certainly not any youths. I had long, anguished conversations with friends, with adults at the Chapel, and with Ike, an adult at Maranatha whom I knew to be an evangelical. Ike expressed sympathy for my concerns but encouraged me to stick with the "staid old ship" and be satisfied with occasional "fresh air" of fellowship when visiting other groups.

I spent hours wandering the fields behind and around our house, talking over my quandary in my head, wanting God to make things clear.

———※———

I wrote a short letter to my parents, leaving it on the kitchen table one morning before I left for high school. I said that I wanted to change churches. They phoned the minister to discuss this development. A few weeks later, they sat me in the kitchen and explained their decision. They would permit me to continue attending events at the Chapel, but I must go to church with them on Sunday mornings and I could not raise this question again for six months. In my fundamentalist circles, we were taught that children had to obey ("submit to") parents, just as wives should submit to husbands—even if parents or husbands were wrong, even if they were not believers. My father said nothing would convince him that I should switch churches: "You are a fanatic. You'll change in a few months." Angry at their decision and their dismissal of my seriousness, I reluctantly agreed to their terms.

Yet I undermined my parents by writing a letter to the Maranatha leadership, addressing them simply as "Gentlemen"—not even pretending politeness by including a "Dear" in the salutation—and asking them to revoke my membership. I worried that my action could prompt punishment from my parents, perhaps rescinding my permission to attend the Chapel. But I felt as if I would explode if I did not speak up. I had to do something. I pointed out that I regarded the congregation—"your church"—as spiritually dead, not "true evangelical," and I no longer subscribed to Christian Reformed doctrine. I was not convinced that Maranatha even constituted a true church. I rejected predestination. The Calvinist experiment, to my mind, had failed. Two elders came to visit and we met in the living room. I knew them—chain-smoking greenhouse farmers, customers of my father's, who swore in Dutch-accented English. I felt defiant and superior.

I am astonished now by how much energy Maranatha put into retaining me. Maranatha co-pastors even contacted my former girlfriend to see whether she might shed light on my behavior. After I eventually became a pastor myself, I never saw a church work that hard to persuade and retain one member.

= =

I read theology: C. S. Lewis, Francis Schaeffer, and A. W. Tozer. More and more I wondered about becoming a pastor. One day I journaled: "I've learned that I am a 'mystic.' Mystics believe that truth or God can be known through spiritual insight." Spiritual insight was what I wanted above all.

After the confrontation with my parents, where they decreed I could not discuss church changing for six months, my sister (sixteen by then) began experiencing strange symptoms—fatigue and odd infections. By June she was diagnosed with leukemia and spent the summer in various hospitals, ending up in Hamilton, an hour's drive away. This crisis consumed our family. My mother spent every day with her. My father and I drove up every other day. I continued as much as possible to participate in the Chapel.

Possibly out of exhaustion, that summer before the six months were up, my parents gave me permission to change churches. "At least you're not joining a weird group, like Jehovah's Witnesses," my father said. "I respect Mennonites. I'm sad you're leaving our church. But I'd be proud if you became a Mennonite pastor."

The Chapel pastor, Peter Loewen, told me that I had to take a membership class and be baptized by immersion. Immersion being the only efficacious means of baptism as they understood it. I balked as I knew that my parents might feel insulted if I were baptized again; they had had me baptized as a child. I also worried about subscribing to Mennonite pacifism, a doctrine that my father found particularly loathsome. But I wanted to join and so assented. Pastor Loewen presented the Mennonite case for baptism and I agreed, the same with the Mennonite peace position.

In years to follow I grew more and more enamored with the peace position. Eventually I did a degree in peace studies at a Mennonite seminary. I attended and organized many peace demonstrations, even getting arrested several times for civil disobedience in opposition to nuclear weapons, against US military interventions in Central America, rejecting the Gulf wars. At an unconscious level I may have been deliberately rejecting my father's cherished ideas. Some people rebel against parents by joining gangs, drinking dangerously, having unprotected sex, doing drugs. I rebelled by becoming Mennonite. Perhaps at a deeper level I was especially attracted to the peace position as a way of countering violence I endured at home.

＝＝

In August, I appeared before the Chapel elders and the next day before gathered members. I was to give my testimony as part of my request for baptism. On both occasions, I spoke for three quarters of an hour. No one told me that testimonies usually take only ten or so minutes. When I was done, a wry member noted: "I'm just glad you're not thirty."

I worried because I never had a born-again conversion—I'd just believed all my life. I had never, as one elder said, "made an experience with the Lord" (English was his second language). The pastor told the congregation, "Arthur is the most outstanding baptismal candidate I ever taught." An adult sponsor of the youth predicted about me: "You will never partake in interdenominational organizations, because you took this change of churches so seriously."

⇒⇐

The church scheduled baptism early on a Sunday morning. It happened to be a weekend when my parents would be away on a brief vacation. They probably would not have wanted to come, so this seemed providential timing. But I felt ambivalence too, part of me wishing they might come after all.

At age nineteen I was immersed in the cold, turbulent waters of Lake Ontario (on the feast of the beheading of St. John the Baptist, no less, although I did not know that at the time). I stood in waves that crested several feet high, where the Niagara River, border between the United States and Canada, empties into that Great Lake. From there I could see the soil of both nations and also, as it happens, historical military forts in both countries. In my baptism into the kingdom of God, I stood apart from those two countries, and apart from their violence and militarism.

On the border, the periphery, of two countries, my baptism declared my primary citizenship not in earthly kingdoms but in God's reign. I am a sojourner, a pilgrim, a resident alien. A Christian's first loyalty is to God's domain.

After the baptism, the congregation held a service of welcoming. I was surprised when men hugged me, some with tears in their eyes. A number of women kissed me on the cheek. I did not know I could feel so loved by a group. One friend there told me, "Never have I seen a member welcomed so warmly into our church." Many adults, the same age as my parents and grandparents, promised prayers of support for me and for my ailing sister Margaret who was struggling against leukemia.

I felt welcomed into my new, alternative family. This was just a week before I would move away to university, bringing my small collection of books, including a copy of an audaciously named volume: *All the Doctrines of the Bible*.

⇒⇐

When my parents returned from their vacation, they did not ask me how the baptism had gone. Nor did I volunteer any account of that momentous weekend.

165

TWENTY-NINE

My father and I enjoyed watching black-and-white films together. Many of them reinforced "old-fashioned" values, our vision of how the world should be. It was usually easy to figure out who were good guys and who were bad. Story endings were clear; good triumphed.

One evening in our living room, filled with sleek teak Danish furniture, we saw *I Want to Live!*, the 1958 film about "Bloody Babs," convicted of a murder that she may or may not have committed. After twists and turns, including a temporary stay at the last minute, she gets executed in a gas chamber. The viewing room is crowded with men—officials, witnesses, reporters—who gawk at her through thick glass windows, watching her perish from cyanide fumes.

My father supported the idea of the death penalty even though Canada had not executed anyone for years and would completely abolish capital punishment in a few more. But the film depiction triggered something for him.

"I don't know," he said afterwards. "That looked horrible. Why do we do such things?"

The next day at breakfast, he offered, "You know, I think maybe the death penalty is wrong. We shouldn't execute people. Ever. I've changed my mind."

"What?" my mom said. "Because of one movie? That's ridiculous."

>=<

Another time, we watched *Suspicion*, an Alfred Hitchcock classic. Joan Fontaine plays a woman who meets charming Johnnie Aysgarth (Cary Grant) on a train and impulsively agrees to marry him. Once wed, she finds out more and more disturbing information about him—an unemployed gambler who lives by borrowing increasing amounts of money and now wants her father's wealth to subsidize his lifestyle. He sells her family's heirlooms to pay off gambling debts. As time passes, his lies grow wilder and wilder. When his good friend dies, Johnnie's fabrications about the circumstances are so outlandish that he becomes suspected of murder.

She discovers that he has been researching poisons and wonders whether Johnnie intends to kill her to solve money woes by inheriting her life insurance. At a key moment in the film he brings her milk before bed. He crosses the main floor, carrying a glass beaker on a silver tray, moving through a heavily shadowed room, his face in darkness, then walking steadily up the stairs.

My father had seen this film before and drew my attention to the scene. "Watch this."

Johnnie steps carefully upward, face unreadable. Light and shadows play. The glass and its contents glow fluorescently. We don't know whether this is innocent milk or something ominous, some kind of poison, arsenic perhaps.

The next morning, over breakfast, my father said, "Wasn't that great? When he walked up the stairs with that glass? We didn't know what to think. Or feel."

Much as I often did not know what to think, feel, or anticipate about him.

When I was sixteen I learned to drive. He let me take the company's bright yellow pickup truck on errands, occasionally to school, or for dates. One week he and my mother went on a Caribbean cruise. My father had just had another heart attack, his second, and he was still in his forties—he needed rest. Opa moved in to look after us for seven days.

On Wednesday evening, I brought my younger sister to a young people's meeting. When I picked her up and backed out of a long narrow gravel driveway, the passenger side's bumper hooked on an inconveniently placed telephone pole. The truck jarred and then swung over to the right with an ominous impact.

Getting out, I saw that the bumper now bent alarmingly outward and the right fender was badly dented. Back at the house, Opa studied the damage and said, "We can't let your father see. He'll be mad. Might have another heart attack." Luckily, my grandfather, still a wheeler-dealer, knew an auto body specialist who agreed to do the repairs within a few days for less than a hundred dollars. The danger of my dad's wrath was averted, for now.

Since the pickup had an extended cab and was longer than usual, it was outfitted with especially large mirrors that jutted out from the doors. Just as I had frequently, years ago, counseled my father not to paint himself into corners, now he regularly told me when I borrowed the truck, "Watch the mirrors."

"I know, Pa," I grumbled, annoyed to be warned about the same thing over and again.

Out in the country, most people got their mail in roadside mailboxes that stood on narrow shoulders close to the pavement. One day the inevitable happened. Driving near Avondale Dairy on Stewart Road, I struck a mailbox with the passenger side mirror. Shattered glass clattered to the ground, the mirror's aluminum frame crumpled.

This time my father was not on vacation, and I dreaded his reaction. Back home, my gut clenching, I found my parents in the living room. Mom had a clinking glass of vermouth and ice, Pa whiskey and ginger ale.

"What's wrong, Artur?" my mom asked. "You look pale."

"I had an accident and hit a mailbox. I busted a mirror. I thought I was careful, paying attention."

To my surprise, my father laughed. "That was bound to happen, son. The way the mirrors stick out, and mailboxes around here so close to the road."

And he laughed again a few months later when, once that mirror was replaced, I hit yet another mailbox.

I never knew what to expect from him. Except to be regularly reminded, "Watch out for the mirrors." And what could I say to that?

※

My sister endured chemo and radiation, a long stay in the hospital, and eventually her disease seemed to be in remission. Yet a year and a half later she caught a minor cold that soon turned into pneumonia and took her life suddenly in the middle of one night, as she lay alone in an oxygen tent at the small hospital in Niagara-on-the-Lake. She was seventeen.

I remembered the words of "St. James Infirmary," sung brilliantly by Louis Armstrong:

> Let her go, let her go
> God bless her
> Wherever she may be

>

＝＝

I was in university by then, two and a half hours away by car, more than three if I took the train instead. I began going home most weekends to visit my folks, so we could console each other. Not so much by words. Mostly by presence. I brought books and notes home to study. My father and I watched films in the evening. My mom fed us: burgers or hot dogs or baked beans on Saturday, roast beef on Sunday.

As is often the case for couples, my parents dealt with their grief differently from each other. My mother and I revisited memories, even funny ones that made us laugh, like the time Margaret somehow accidentally flipped a plate full of spaghetti and meatballs through our living room, a red stain stretching the length of the green wall-to-wall carpeting.

My father never said anything about Margaret, except occasionally to note his surprise that we could tell stories about her. He never did and did not laugh at shared memories. He could not even utter Margaret's name for months. Grief made him more quiet than usual. But he did say, "It would have been easier if she had never been born."

That hard-hearted idea bothered me back then. Now I suspect his emotions were unbearable. Deep pain rendered him almost speechless.

＝＝

Until the day he died, I never knew what to make of his unsettling silences.

When I was in my early thirties, my parents joined my wife and me and our small children at a borrowed cottage for a few days. I saw again his antisocial eccentricity. On Monday, he and I sat alone for a while at a table outside the cottage, high up on a dune, overlooking Georgian Bay. I told him about our life, the church I pastored, the children. He was completely quiet. Didn't look at me. Didn't respond. Yet, like that baby reaching for the photo, I still longed for connection. He looked away, smoking, sipping his whiskey and ginger ale.

My mom reported that he often did the same with her, sometimes surly and silent for entire weekends. The day after that nonconversation, my parents' friends, Oom Al and Tante Anke, invited them sailing for an afternoon. Pa wanted to bring a book or magazine to have something to do. We talked him out of it—that time. But other sailing trips with them he spent entire excursions reading down in the boat's cabin, ignoring the scenery and the conversations.

＝＜

In Pilsen, the inner-city Chicago neighborhood where my wife, Lorna, and I lived for a few years, we frequently heard nearby gunfire. The police often did not respond when we phoned, even though they had a station blocks away. One subzero winter week, in the alley of the next block, sanitation workers found a frozen baby in a trash can. Drug pushers walked around with pagers to better serve customers. When the streetlights went out, we knew a deal was going down nearby. This was a long way from rural St. Davids, population 500.

My father and I had argued politics ever since I went to university and changed my mind about so many issues. I opposed colonialism, supported socialism, resisted warmaking, defended unions. Now when I phoned him in Canada, he'd say. "What a great president you folks have."

"Are you kidding? Tax cuts are hard on folks. We know people who are being evicted. Who can't afford lawyers. Kids have days where they don't eat."

"That's tough. But taxes are too high. That discourages business."

And another familiar theme: "Besides, Reagan stands up to communists. That's what we need."

"Who cares about communists? People in our church are hungry. They don't have jobs. They live in hovels."

"They should work harder."

He phoned once, though, trying to find something in common. "Isn't it great how Americans and Russians are working to free those whales stuck in the ice near Alaska?"

I understood what he was attempting—to establish at least one opinion in common—but I could not concede. "Whales? What about the poor people in our neighborhood? Why not save them?"

My parents visited over Christmas. With their help, we had purchased an old home, a former dairy, on West 21st Street. Our two-story gray Insulbrick house leaned against the three-flat next door. Our children's toys rolled by themselves from one end of the sloping kitchen floor to the other.

My dad decided to go for a walk, moving carefully because hollow sidewalks in our neighborhood were cracked and often collapsed. People threw furniture—old chairs and disintegrating couches—into the holes. Pa stepped over broken glass that seemed to be everywhere. He watched police harass teenagers on a sidewalk around the corner. He smelled charred beams of houses gutted by flames. Dirty-faced children played with broken plastic toys, dashing into the busy street. Cars with cracked windshields, without license plates, missing bumpers, roared by, unmuffled. Two cars collided at high speed in one intersection, fenders and bumpers flying and clanging to the pavement; both drivers—probably undocumented, certainly uninsured—exited their cars and ran in separate directions down the streets. My dad counted the bars, often two or three to an intersection. Graffiti covered exposed walls and traffic signs. Young men slouched against buildings and asked for money.

When he returned, he said, "You know, all the communists would have to do to make really good propaganda is walk around your neighborhood with a film camera, even a black-and-white one. They wouldn't need to add commentary."

After returning to Canada, he continued to ponder the poverty, dereliction, and neglect he'd seen. He had gotten acquainted with hungry people in our congregation, saw how hard they worked, and no longer blamed them for their poverty. He remembered church children who visited our house, and he could not bear to think about their suffering. At parties he argued heatedly with his friends (all of them Dutch immigrant businessmen), he the only one to question Ronald Reagan's accomplishments. He was no longer convinced that tax cuts were necessarily good. Inequality, he saw, was not just a result of laziness.

That winter, my parents went to Florida on vacation and invited us to join them. Lorna and I worked stressful jobs that didn't pay much—she as a nurse and me in the inner-city congregation. So we appreciated a parent-subsidized luxury holiday. I drove out to nature reserves in early mornings to watch birds. One day, driving back, I heard on the local NPR station that Stevie Ray Vaughan, the legendary Texas rock-blues guitarist, would play that evening in Tampa. Stevie Ray, imagine that—one of my favorite performers then, and now, only forty miles away.

I found Lorna and my folks drinking coffee by the hotel swimming pool, overlooking the blue Gulf. I excitedly reported the news, angling for company. But Lorna wanted to relax with my mom. "I'll go," said my dad. I went to phone for tickets.

We left in the late afternoon, both of us preferring to get to destinations early—the Dutch priority of punctuality. In Tampa, we stopped to eat at a diner a few blocks from the concert venue, sitting in a booth beside tall windows that looked out over the business section of town, streets quiet now that the workday was done. We ordered comfort food, a Reuben sandwich for me and hot beef for him, both of us dousing fries with ketchup. We sat, sipped weak American beer, and said little during the meal, so I studied the eccentric customers. A drunken man perched precariously on a stool and called across the room to the waitress, Madge. An elderly woman sat at a table alone. Madge addressed her as "Mrs. Wicker." A middle-aged man in a rumpled suit, a salesman perhaps, huddled at a table loaded with beer bottles. I had the impression that all three lonely-looking people ate there regularly, perhaps every day.

Then my father and I walked the quarter mile to the auditorium, its cement block halls echoing like a high school gym. We sat eight rows from the stage. Worrying what my opinionated father might think, I felt disconcerted by burly bikers, tattooed and fierce-looking, both men and women. Leather jackets and bandanas. Graying ponytails and torn, grease-stained jeans. Many arrived well-lubricated, swaying as they walked, sliding low in their seats.

The concert began with the Fabulous Thunderbirds, a band led by Kim Wilson, one of the finest blues harmonica players then and now, and Jimmie Vaughan, an amazing guitarist and Stevie Ray's older brother. The Thunderbirds blended rockabilly and Texas blues to perform some of the liveliest rhythms I ever heard. I wanted to dance. Not just me. Bikers stood in place swaying, piling into aisles, bumping bodies against each other, and surging to the front, beneath the stage and bouncing, throwing up arms, whistling and yelling.

I fretted: What did my father think?

More and more people rolled and lit crooked, stubby cigarettes, inhaled deeply, emitted clouds of smoke, and passed around the twisted and bent glowing paper cylinders, the room filling with autumn scents of burning leaves. My dad the businessman—probably the oldest person in the room, certainly the most respectable—spent as much time studying the audience as watching the band. Finally, he turned, elbowed me, and asked, a little too loudly for my comfort, "Is that marijuana?" I answered affirmatively, although I didn't want to say how I knew.

I had never paid attention to the Thunderbirds before but became an instant fan. Recognizing the talent and rejoicing in their exquisite rhythms, I felt torn. Aside from seeing my father's fingers drumming—I hoped in appreciation not impatience—I had no idea what he thought. My worries about his opinions distracted me.

Then Stevie Ray. I had heard him live several times by then (he would die in his mid-thirties in a helicopter accident between gigs a few years later). This show stunned. Joy and longing, ecstasy and yearning, grief and delight exploded from the strings he played. If he had given an altar call, inviting us to pretty much anything, even dissolute living, I might have leapt forward and joined those dancing bikers. But I only allowed my body to bounce a little in my seat. I did not want to be too weird in front of my father. Yet euphoria tried to erupt within, a predictable result for me when minor keys mate with driving rhythms. I held back.

Pa remained unresponsive, showing no emotions. He never looked at me, although I glanced often at his impassive face, trying to read it.

When the concert ended, we walked in silence back to the rental car. I had witnessed two astonishing performances but had not enjoyed either, unable to let loose and release anxiety about what went on in my father's head. The evening a waste, a write-off. Why did I bother?

"What did you think, Pa?"

"Not bad," he told me. We said little else during the forty-minute drive back to our hotel, breathing in salty air that wafted from the nearby Gulf through our car windows.

The next morning, still trying to sort it all out. I was reading Raymond

Chandler, *The Long Goodbye*, and drank coffee outside at a small table under an umbrella, beside the pool. My father sat there too, smoking and sipping coffee, newspaper in hand.

After a time, he looked over and said: "About last night."

"Yeah?" wondering what might come.

"Do you remember all those people dancing in the aisles and up at the front?"

"Yeah." O Lord, what would he say about high and drunkenly dishevelled revellers?

"When I was a young man in the Netherlands, I went every year to the jazz festival in Den Haag. Wouldn't miss it. When the music got really good, *I* danced in the aisles."

I wish I had known the night before. I might have enjoyed myself. Maybe even danced.

THIRTY

My father never expressed regrets, even as I fumbled questions the last months of his life.

In January 1991 an oncologist told him that he had his third bout of cancer.

"I'll fight it again," my dad asserted.

"I'm afraid this time it's terminal. No cure or remission. The best we can do is help with the pain."

"How long do I have?"

"Hard to say. Months maybe. But not a year."

My dad called that doctor's appointment his "death sentence," although he was trying to attract a smile, not pity. He did not say much else. Except for this: "I hope to see spring flowers and blossoms once more." I was intrigued: this from the man who preferred that greenhouse farmers raise vegetables.

In my early thirties at the time, he thirty years older, by then Lorna, the children, and I lived four hours away and our family began driving to Niagara several times a month. Pa liked seeing the "little people," Erin age six and Paul just turned four.

I studied him in the family room. "What are you staring at?" he sometimes asked. But I said nothing, unwilling to explain that I was trying to memorize what he looked like.

Occasionally, I raised questions.

"How do you feel now about smoking?" My father's cancer, first in his throat, then in his lungs, and finally tendriled to bones and brain, likely had to do with the fierce two- to possibly three-pack-a-day cigarette habit that he'd had for over forty years.

"Do you wish you took more time off from the business?"

"Looking back, what would you change?"

"What do you regret?"

He always responded the same, "It's too late to think about that now."

I wanted to ask about his anger, the damage he did, but this seemed impolite, bad form, and, besides, I had no idea how to begin. We mostly sat in silence in my parents' family room. I studied him from the side, his head propped on his arm and face in his palm (still trying to cover his weak chin), smoking, almost always smoking, still smoking, reading a book or a newspaper, near to hand a low-cut glass containing Johnnie Walker, ginger ale, and ice, maybe watching professional wrestling or a World War II film. I tried to frame questions. I hoped for some signal of remorse, especially toward me, but that never came.

≥≤

When I was a child, my parents often demanded apologies for interrupting adults in conversation, speaking of an adult as "he" or "she" rather than using name or title, forgetting to say please or thank you. But never did my father apologize, not for shattering the car while drunk, not for shattering his fancy new camera on the living room floor and grinding the glass lens into the olive green wall-to-wall carpeting one Sunday afternoon, not for shattering an alarm clock by hurling it at my mother in their bedroom where it embedded itself into the closet door and crystal scattered over the floor.

And not for shattering me. As far as I know, he never beat anyone else. That also grieves me. Why did I get singled out in this way? What made me special?

≥≤

Around the time of his final diagnosis, he and I still contended over politics, this time about the first Gulf War. He felt Americans were justified in attacking Iraq. I did not. But we did not argue with as much heat as before, resigning ourselves to different sides. We had more immediate matters to address.

Over the months he steadily lost his appetite and weight. My mother insisted he drink Ensure.

In the spring, peach trees blossomed and tulips raised themselves from the ground, all of them early that year. My father's hope fulfilled, one small mercy, maybe even a miracle.

He had continued to drive to work every weekday, month after month. The first Friday of May, he put in a day's work, as he had done all week, working, as it turns out, until almost the end of his life. Lorna, the kids, and I arrived that evening for the weekend. My father moved gingerly but still declined his cane. Friday evening and all day Saturday, he stayed on the couch, saying little. He seemed—if possible—more withdrawn than ever.

On Saturday, I went into Niagara-on-the-Lake to pick up his prescription. The sun shone and tourists strolled sidewalks, licking ice cream cones and laughing. "How," I wondered, "can the world go on as normal and people still enjoy themselves while my father is dying?"

On Sunday, he remained in bed. I stayed the day with him in my parents' bedroom. I don't remember what we watched on TV except the commercial that showed peaches, glistening like gold and sliced into vanilla ice cream.

"Oh," I sighed. "Nothing better than fresh peaches in the summer."

My father did not respond and I immediately regretted my words, feeling idiotic. He likely would never again enjoy fresh peaches.

Monday morning the doctor visited. As he was leaving, near the front door, he told my mother and me: "Well, I can't say. Could be months, could be weeks."

My parents both hoped he could stay at home as long as possible, maybe even die there; my mother was always haunted by the fact that both her daughter and her father died unexpectedly in the middle of the night, alone in hospital rooms a couple miles away. I began planning how to divide time between Windsor, where I was pastoring, and Niagara to help my mother care for my dad. I phoned electronics stores, inquiring about purchasing or renting a second Macintosh computer for Niagara, so I could work both places on sermons and correspondence.

Erin was scheduled to be a panther in a class play in Windsor on Monday evening. Since we wanted her life to have some normalcy, I would take her, Lorna and Paul remaining behind. I said goodbye to my dad. Seeing my somber and earnest visage, he told me, "Don't worry. I'll be here when you get back."

I thought that Erin understood what was going on, that she was old enough to handle bad news. As we rode on the high arch of the Garden City Skyway Bridge, over the Welland Canal, I began: "Erin, we need to talk about Opa."

"I know. He's sick."

"He's very sick, Erin."

"Yeah."

I thought she knew where this was going, that she understood.

"He's not going to live. He's going to die."

She disconnected her seatbelt and flung herself to the floor, howling. Once we were off the bridge, I pulled the car onto the shoulder, reached over, put my arms around her, and consoled her as best I could.

⇒⇐

Erin's play went well and we stayed the night at our house in Windsor. It turned out that that evening was also the last time my father spoke, I learned the next day. By the time we got back, Tuesday afternoon, he was mute.

"It's me, Pa," I said, leaning over him. His bright blue eyes held mine but there was no way of telling whether he heard me, whether he understood. He did not explicitly acknowledge me. "I hope you're OK." No response to that either. Long used to his silences, I had not realized that they could worsen.

Now we needed to change our strategy, to pace ourselves. The days ahead would be taxing and we did not know how long Pa would live. I insisted that evening that my mother should rest. She had been busy with him for the last few months. She reluctantly agreed.

I spent the night with my father, lying beside him in their queen-size bed as he restlessly struggled, trying to sleep. He grunted when he needed the washroom. I escorted him. After he had done the necessaries, I wiped his privates, the first time I had ever seen him naked, and wondered how he felt about this latest indignity. I had changed my own children often and recalled my mother telling me that not once in his life did my father change a diaper.

Then I walked him back to bed. Lorna waited on the landing outside the room, "Is everything OK?"

I went out and whispered, "I feel bad, holding my dad's arm, and propping him up when he walks. What about his pride? What if he wants to do it on his own?"

"You have to hold him. It's too dangerous for him to fall."

I was learning to care for my dying father, expecting this apprenticeship to last months.

I lay beside him again, murmuring encouragement. He was restless during the night. I spoke in Dutch, hoping this consoled him, although I was unsure.

In the morning, the doctor paid another visit shortly after breakfast. "It's hard to know," he said. "Could be days, or weeks. He doesn't seem to be in pain. That's good."

Lorna, my mother, and I took turns sitting by him. An hour after the doctor departed, Lorna left Pa's side to find my mother and me sitting in the kitchen, drinking tea. Lorna, a nurse, told us that the time approached; his breath was accelerating, his toes and fingers turning blue and cooling, a sign that his circulation was shutting down.

The three of us gathered by the bed. Watching. Lorna and I on one side. My mother across from us. My mom took a hand and stroked his nicotine-stained fingers. I held his other limp hand, the one that had hit me in fury two decades before, but never again.

"We love you, Pa," I said.

His breath sped, deep gulps and shudders, and within an hour he was gone.

The longest silence ever.

＝＝

The funeral was held at Covenant, the newest Christian Reformed church in the area, and I told the story of my father and Stevie Ray. We sang "By the Sea of Crystal." Our funeral convoy traveled to the Lakeshore Road cemetery in Niagara-on-the-Lake. We made our way to the graves of my grandmother, grandfather, and sister. Now my father would lie here too. You know this country is home when more and more loved ones are buried here.

I remember many of those attending. Especially moved that members of my congregation traveled four hours to come and that a number of Mennonite ministers also drove long distances to support me. My dad's cousin

Art was there. In his mid-forties he had just suffered a massive and almost fatal stroke. He insisted on leaving the hospital early so he could be present. He still had a large bandage wrapped around his head.

Beside the open grave, as is the custom of Dutch Calvinists, Reverend Vos invited us to recite together the Apostles' Creed.

> *I believe . . .*
> *In the communion of the saints.*
> *The forgiveness of sins.* His and mine.
> *The resurrection of the body.* His and mine.
> *The life everlasting.* His and mine.

My Mennonite colleagues told me that this moment especially moved them. They did not think any of their members could say this creed by heart.

⇒⇐

Unrelenting grief rocked me, engulfing waves of emotional pain that I had not felt since my sister died—familiar, but not welcome. Not this again, I told myself. Please, no.

After the bustle of funeral preparations and the funeral itself, we returned to Windsor, trying to resume regular lives.

One evening, after everyone was in bed, I went to our front porch, sitting in the dark on a small bench, trying to take in the permanent loss.

I noticed a neighbor across the street returning from her shift as a nurse at a Detroit hospital. She fascinated me, both her tall hourglass figure wrapped in bright red and orange, and her shaved head, uncommon for women at that time. I watched her unlock the front door of her house and enter. She closed her door. Through its window I could see her hall light snap off.

Suddenly I was overcome with grief, hunched over and weeping. Trying to hold in my noise. Worrying about making a scene in view of my neighbors.

⇒⇐

Glass greenhouses are never more beautiful than just prior to completion, but they also are especially unbearable then. Sparkling panes admit such quantities of sunlight that their steel pipe and angle iron skeletons shine. Before ventilation is installed, humidity and heat build up so that working inside reminds me of afterlife threats I used to hear in Sunday sermons.

Almost no plants—other than cacti—can bear such furnace conditions, so farmers cover hothouses with streaky whitewash for months, just to diminish the sun's effects. Glass surfaces turn opaque. Standing outside one seldom knows what grows inside, whether flowers or potted plants, produce or greens.

When my father died, I thought I had achieved a measure of peace with him and in our relationship. Gradually in those final months I resigned myself to the idea that some gaps never get crossed. I loved him and felt sure that he loved me too. I needed nothing more. He would not let me see inside him and I could live without doing so.

A few years after his death, I attended a denominational event near his last home. I felt distracted amid all the debates and discussions, and I never liked big groups. So I got in my car and drove. I saw the house where he died—my mother had married again and moved elsewhere by then. I noted greenhouses, including ones I helped build. I slowed down past my high school and junior high and the place where we lived when I was a teen. I remembered how my father let loose on fourteen-year-old me there, with fists and feet knocking me down and when I rose knocking me down again. Finally pummeling me with apples that tumbled out of a glass fruit bowl that he smashed. I wandered over to the red Insulbrick place that we lived in before that—it was covered in aluminum siding now—the place where he battered seven-year-old me into a blackout. I stopped at the cemetery where he lay beside my grandfather, my grandmother, and my sister. I wiped my eyes steadily that day.

I realized that I never understood my father, our relationship, or even myself—many of my explanations nothing more than whitewash.

> "The air filled with
> flying glass, I hardly knew what I
> said or who I would be now that I had forgiven you."
>
> (Sharon Olds)*

* Sharon Olds, "After 37 Years My Mother Apologizes for My Childhood," in *The Gold Cell* (New York: Alfred A. Knopf, 1994), 43.

Sometimes people ask, "Have you forgiven your father?" Sometimes they are devout Christians and I hear an implicit "should" in their question. Sometimes they are more therapeutically oriented and I am not clear about their agenda.

No matter. I never know how to answer. Forgive? What does that mean? Obviously, I have not forgotten. Nor have I dismissed what happened as unimportant. I have found a measure of what I consider forgiveness. I understand something of the violence in him. I know he dialed down the brutality that he was taught and that he imbibed and that was reinforced by his exposure to two wars.

I am sad and wounded by his actions and choices. I wish that these things never happened. But I do not hold them against him. I did love him and did help in taking care of him when he died. That was not hard to do. Having finally, with this book, named what he did, I now want to release his debts and look forward to our reuniting by the sea of crystal.

THIRTY-ONE

Recently, I dreamed of standing in the skeleton of a storm-battered greenhouse. Glass panes fractured by high winds and hurtling hail lay scattered across dirt.

Over a half century ago I started working in greenhouse construction, cleaning up and disposing of glittering shards every morning. Tidying work sites, making them safe. My father paid me a quarter for each morning's effort. Friends worked for their parents on nearby family farms by gathering fruit from vines and trees; I picked dangerous garbage from the ground.

I did not use gloves; men and boys never did. My fingers and palms bled. I gradually learned how to grasp glass and reduce the risk of cuts. I felt good about my ability to retrieve fragments, angling them in my fingers, holding them loosely in my palm until gathering enough glittering jagged pieces to dump into empty five-gallon putty cans still sticky with gray goop. To this day, when glass breaks, even before brooms and dustpans appear, I am among the first to kneel and begin cleaning up. I like corralling glass.

In my dream, glass poked, pricked, and penetrated my thin-soled slippers. I pulled them off and pried at pointed pieces, blood spotting the surface of my skin. No sooner did I remove one splinter than another jabbed me. I could not work fast enough; slivers insistently porcupined my feet, liquid crimson threading the padded whorls of my soles.

Such dreams do not surprise me.

My father felt bad when hail or wind caused disasters for farmers, his customers, but shattered glass also meant insurance work and good income for him. In that dream of the skeletal greenhouse, denuded by a storm, his crew, in ragged paint-stained clothes, cleans up debris, preparing to reglaze the stripped structure. Nothing surprising here.

Except when, holding an empty putty container, I offer, "I could help, Pa."

My father had often doubted whether my studies or later my activism qualified as worthy work, at times calling me "semi-intellectual" or "pinko." But in the dream he dissuaded me from tending this latest catastrophe.

"That's OK, Son. Don't worry about it."

He often called me Son, the memory still echoing. I wish I could hear him say it again, at least once.

Even as my hands itch to begin, I obey. Over fifty years later, they still know how to handle shattered glass, but I don't need to do that anymore. Mishaps no longer benefit him. And he stopped breaking things long ago. His fists and feet no longer launch out in fury, nor are they directed at me.

Only in dreams do he and I ponder picking up the remaining fragments.

※

A few years after my father died, the musical group Enigma released a video for a song called "Return to Innocence." An old man falls dead; then his life plays in reverse. Fallen fruit floats from the ground and returns to branches. Broken bread reassembles. Timbered trees raise themselves. A dry dog shakes itself and becomes wet again. A smashed bottle on the floor pops up and comes together mid-air to be caught by the child who dropped it.

If only it were so.

THIRTY-TWO

Two things immediately impressed me about the hurricane candle holder, a stained-glass cylinder, one foot tall and four inches across, designed to accommodate a single taper and protect it from drafts.

Its theme was blue irises, the top rim jagged with their petals and leaves. Irises are Lorna's favorite flower. She raises them around our yard every place that we live. I buy her iris bouquets on special occasions.

And the opalescent glass and black leaded seams evoked a Tiffany lamp style. Lorna loves Tiffany too.

I gladly gave this perfect gift for her birthday.

A few months later, as a Mennonite pastor at the time, I planned to preach on a famous verse, "Let your light shine before others, so that they may see your good works and give glory to your Father in heaven."

Since congregants responded well to sermon visuals, I asked Lorna about borrowing this candle-lamp. I thought a quivering burst of light behind colored glass could convey the meaning of demonstrating God's love, mercy, and grace. She agreed and I situated it atop a high pedestal beside the pulpit, to be visible to a hundred or more people, even those in the back row.

I knew visuals should be tested ahead of time and on Friday I dutifully set an eight-inch taper inside the candle-lamp and lit it. When I walked to the back of the room, however, I could not actually see a flame; the single candle cast very little light. I found five more tapers and set them in the candle-lamp too. I lit them and moved to the back, glad to watch blue irises and green leaves glow, light flickering. All set for Sunday, I doused the candles.

Two days later, I lit them midway through my sermon, confident that this tiny gesture would be memorable and persuasive, especially for those who process visually. As often happens with preaching, congregants would remember something all right. But not what I intended.

After the sermon, I proceeded with the rest of the service, letting translucent Tiffany irises continue to share their beauty with the congregation. During the pastoral prayer, though, something happened that I had never encountered in all my years as a pastor. A congregational stalwart, Elaine, a serious and unsmiling Christian who always sat near the front and scrutinized my theology to determine whether I might be a heretic, interrupted my prayer midsentence. "Your display is melting, Arthur!" she called.

I opened an eye at the unexpected heckling and glanced right, startled to see my beautiful gift to Lorna might soon disintegrate in front of the congregation. Leaded seams had started to liquify and begun to run. I imagined glass pieces shifting, some falling down, abandoned shards, shattered glass; the cylinder could take on the shape of a bowing pear, totally collapsing.

I had not realized that massed candles could generate that much heat.

I hastily said "Amen" and walked over to the pedestal to blow out the flames. I looked to the back where Lorna sat with our children, wondering how she would feel about what I did to her prized gift. The hot cylinder continued to steam through the final hymn and then the benediction; meanwhile hazardous lead fumes drifted through the sanctuary.

After the service, I went to the foyer to greet departing worshipers, something I did every week. Speaking and visiting with familiar folks, I tried to pretend that I was not worried about anything—something else I did every Sunday morning. Then Sharon appeared, one of our more independent thinkers, an artist in her mid-thirties.

"I work with stained glass," she told me. "I went up and looked. I'm sure I can fix that." Relieved, I arranged for her to take it, hoping that she could restore the piece.

⸎

Sharon loves stained glass, enjoying the play of light, glowing tones, unexpected glimpses of beauty in brokenness. She assembles fragments into abstract collages of colors, creating mosaics. She adheres copper strips to shards and then, with melted lead, joins them. This finicky, time-consuming work takes practice, both learning how to cut glass and to place pieces.

Repairing stained glass—as she now offered to do—is more difficult than creating something new. She tells me that most people do not realize the hazards. Glass does not always cooperate with diamond-headed cutters, certainly not dividing smoothly or purposefully as paper does between a scissors' blades. And pieces can swiftly injure the assembler, with hard-to-mend angles slicing deeply beneath the skin. Corrosive chemicals needed for this work and the lead that is melted for soldering both cause toxic fumes.

Assemble, or reassemble, then, at your own risk.

———

In her workshop, she removed the melted lead tears and streaks and smoothed all the joints. A few months later, she presented us with the refurbished Tiffany-iris candleholder, delivered in a shoebox, cradled in white tissue. It was as beautiful as we remembered. Lorna and I could not see that it had ever been damaged at all.

THIRTY-THREE

In my mid-thirties, two decades after the last time my father beat me, and two years after he died, I broke glass twice in one week. Once, for the first time in my life, in anger.

On a September Saturday, atop a stepladder, I was scraping the peeling wood around our garage window, preparing it for painting later that month. I thought about long to-do lists at home with our small children and at the rural church I pastored, which was suddenly attracting newcomers who squeezed our small space, not to mention our comfort zone. In a couple of hours I was to head to a Christian education conference where I would give a workshop on spirituality. Plus, this window needed work. On top of it all I was to leave for a five-day retreat in forty-eight hours.

Overwhelmed by an impossibly long list of duties that was complicated by my upcoming trip, a cloud of steamy mist descended into my brain and swirled behind my eyes. I grunted in frustration and plunged my fist against the window, startled by how little resistance the glass offered, how easily it fractured, like the thinnest ice. I could have pushed my fist through, no punch necessary. The cascade of jagged accusers clattered to the ground. I felt relief that I had not cut myself, as such an injury would be hard to explain, especially to parishioners. I fetched a broom and dustpan from the kitchen.

As I stepped back into the garage, my mother pulled up; she had just completed the ninety-minute drive for a prearranged weekend visit. She saw the broken window and scattered glass. I averted my face from her.

"*Is het weer zo?*" she asked. "Is it happening again?" She remembered my father.

With nothing to say, I finished cleaning up the debris, then went in, showered, changed into good clothes, and put on a tie. I drove to the conference, held in a local high school gym, where Sunday school teachers listened to me claim that prayer can de-stress our lives (and the irony was not lost on me). On the way home, I stopped at a hardware store and spent the day's honorarium on a replacement pane that the proprietor cut to size, along with a can of gray putty, glazing nails, and a putty knife. Back home, placing and securing that window, I remembered that my father glazed for years but never repaired his own rage-inflicted destruction.

≡≡

On Monday, I went to stay with Henri Nouwen, a priest whose books had influenced my prayer life and ministry. He resided an hour's drive away, just north of Toronto at Daybreak, part of L'Arche, a worldwide network of communities where people with developmental and intellectual challenges live with their assistants. I had interviewed Nouwen for a magazine several years earlier, and then visited a couple times. Now he would guide me on a five-day retreat. He told me that duration was "quite short," yet it was the longest retreat I'd ever taken. I could not imagine a longer one, given home and church responsibilities.

I knew Henri was speaking at a nearby seminary so, as expected, when I arrived at his house, no one was there. I found my room and was welcomed by a warm note and vase of bright sunflowers that testified to his love for Van Gogh. Minutes later he phoned, apologizing for not being there for my arrival. I was glad to hear his familiar Dutch accent, the one that consoles and reassures me. He said he'd given me the "best room."

That first evening, through my open door, he saw me reading, and said, "You better get a nice lamp. This one is so awful." He went down the hall and in minutes showed up with one that he'd retrieved from his room. A while later, he returned, handing me a CD player and disks, Bach's *Brandenburg Concertos*, Beethoven's *Moonlight Sonata*, Mozart symphonies, Vivaldi's *Four Seasons*. "Play these as loud as you like," he told me. "I won't mind."

Every day we met twice for an hour to discuss Scripture passages that he assigned for my meditation, insisting I use his Jerusalem Bible. Pondering those texts, my week's mantra emerged from Mary's Magnificat: "The Almighty has done great things for me."

We ate breakfast together and later in the day drank tea that he prepared. Once we went to a cozy Austrian restaurant nearby; the proprietors knew him well. Our meal—tender red cabbage simmered in apples, nutmeg, and cloves, *Sauerbraten* with sweetly tangy gravy, followed by strong coffee with real whipping cream—reminded us of Dutch cooking.

On my second day, we went to his office, at the front of the Daybreak property. He showed me shelves of his published books. "Just take whatever," he told me, giving me three copies of the Dutch translation of his Prodigal Son book, *Eindelijk Thuis*, "Finally Home," the title naming a yearning that he and I both shared.

Another evening, he arrived back at the house around 10 p.m. I was in a chair, illuminated by his lamp, reading with my feet propped on the bed. He sat down on the mattress and gave my legs a friendly pat. We each reviewed our day for the other.

⇒⇐

Henri explained that he'd made sure his calendar that week had plenty of space for our conversations. I knew this was no small thing, given his responsibilities and long to-do lists.

Why, I asked, when he had many other commitments? He said, "We've built up a relationship and know each other. And you have the stamina to do your thing without being intrusive or demanding." I thought about that, saying nothing, then he added, "By the way, I don't want you to pay anything to Daybreak for this stay. You are here as my friend."

All week, I struggled with whether to tell him about that window. It felt ridiculous and humiliating. Every time I came to Daybreak, I seemed to be in crisis. During my first visit, an hour-long interview turned into a daylong conversation, and Henri addressed my evident stress. Toward the end of our time together, he pulled a chair near and leaned toward me, explaining, "You have a tender heart. This means that God is calling you to a deep spiritual life. Tenderness can destroy you because you can just be pulled apart, burn out, and the whole thing. But you can also be a mystic. That's what you obviously have to be."

"What does that mean?" I asked.

"To be a mystic I don't mean anything more than that God is the one who loves you deeply. And that's what you have to trust. And keep trusting, keep trusting, keep trusting."

On this most recent visit, I evasively summarized my recent days of feeling once again "overloaded" and "stressed." I couldn't bear to confess the broken glass, even when he said, "Our time together will be helpful only if you are completely honest."

⇉⇇

Each morning, we prayed with a Carmelite breviary. I kept losing my place in it and Henri helped me find my way. After the formal prayers, we sat for thirty minutes of silence. He concluded our time by kneeling and stretching out his hands and reciting aloud, from memory, Charles de Foucauld's prayer:

> Father,
> I abandon myself into your hands;
> Do with me what you will.
> Whatever you may do, I thank you;
> I am ready for all, I accept all.
> Let only your will be done in me,
> And in all your creatures.
> I wish no more than this,
> O Lord.
> Into your hands I commend my soul;
> I offer it to you with all the love
> of my heart,
> for I love you, Lord,
> and so need to give myself,
> to surrender myself into your hands,
> without reserve
> and with boundless confidence.
> For you are my Father.

After morning prayers we breakfasted on buttered rye toast and thin Gouda slices—I had brought him a Dutch cheese plane as a gift—and Henri boiled milk for our coffee. We chatted, aware that within the hour L'Arche community members and assistants would arrive for Mass.

At one breakfast, Henri told me that I needed to make my ministry "more eucharistic," but I had no idea what he meant. Our church celebrated the Supper only a few times a year. I didn't ask for clarification though. I felt I should know. Later that day, he gave me a manuscript of a forthcoming book, *With Burning Hearts: A Meditation on the Eucharistic Life*. From it I learned that in the Eucharist Jesus *takes* us, *blesses* us, then *breaks* us, and, finally, *gives* us into ministry.

⇒⇐

At the end of Thursday's breakfast, Henri stood: "I need to make a quick phone call." He paused, then said, "Oh. Can you clean these for me?" He gestured toward two simple glass candleholders on the counter, streaked by discolored wax that had dripped and accumulated along the sides.

"Sure. *Ik moet iets doen voor de kost.*" ("I have to do something for room and board.") One at a time, I held each holder over the garbage bin. With a butter knife I pried and scraped away large wax chunks. Then I removed remaining bits with my thumbnail. Finally, I filled the dishpan with warm water and immersed the first, scrubbing and setting it aside on a kitchen towel, before doing the same for the second.

Drying them, I was shocked to see cracks in one. But how? I thought I had handled them carefully, set them down gently. Had the fracture been there before and I overlooked it? Surely I would have noticed? Is this how I repay Henri's hospitality? What would he say? He cherished nice things.

Cheryl, a community assistant, wandered through the kitchen. "Look," I told her. "Somehow this cracked. I don't know whether I did it, but I feel bad. They're pretty simple. They can't be worth much."

"Unfortunately," she said, "they are. A famous glass blower in Vermont custom-made them for Henri."

My stomach tightened over this mishap. I worried about his disapproval or worse. I could hardly sit still as I waited. Minutes later, he burst into the kitchen, hurrying to get to the basement.

"Wait, Henri, I have to show you something."

"Okay, but I don't have much time. I must get ready. The service is in a few minutes."

"I'm not sure what happened. Whether I did it or not. But one holder is cracked. I'm sorry. I thought I was careful."

He grew very still, no longer in a rush. He looked toward the counter and turned the glass stem in his hands, studying the damage. I waited, fret-

192

ting about his reaction. Would he scold and tell me about its value, its specialness, its uniqueness? Would he question whether I was careful enough? Would he lament the loss of something precious and valuable? Would he raise his voice? Would this ruin—even end—my visit, perhaps all future visits? Would he ask, as my father often did, "What's wrong with you?"

"Oh, Artur," he said, for his accent, like my father's, always mispronounced my name. "It's OK. Don't worry." Pulling me from my kitchen chair, his long arms swept me into a bear hug, tight against his chest, full body contact. I could count each bony finger pressed into my back. Seconds later he released me and then disappeared, descending noisily to the basement chapel, bouncing down the wooden steps. All went so fast that I hardly knew what had happened.

I went to brush my teeth, hoping to calm myself. Then I too hustled down the stairway planks. I settled into the gentle sway of an IKEA armchair, one where I had meditated on Scripture texts every morning and afternoon that week. Assistants and members arrived, unwrapping blankets, positioning wheelchairs, murmuring encouragements, arranging large pillows for contorted bodies, massaging backs and shoulders.

I knew what to expect: informal eucharistic liturgy and simple songs that involved and included people with severe handicaps, some of them periodically moaning. I would savor Taizé chants and the upcoming homey and holy worship.

I looked at the low-slung altar. Made of highly polished wood and shaped like a boat, an ark, a safe haven in turbulent times. It had been commissioned by Henri for this space.

From behind it, Henri, in white alb and emerald stole, flung his arms right and left, embracing the gathering, and calling, "The Lord be with you."

My eyes ran to and fro at his ambidextrous invitation and were drawn to the candles. The holders, each bearing one lit taper, stood at attention on either end of the altar. Studying the small sentinels, I could no longer see where that break might be.

THIRTY-FOUR

The room overlooks a river that maps hereabouts call the South Branch of the Muskoka, a twisting liquid sinew that relentlessly flows over granite layers, some a billion years old. It starts at the wonderfully named Lake of Bays, eventually emptying into Georgian Bay.

New neighbors—they have a Dutch surname, but I haven't met them yet—put up a sign that dubs their shoreside refuge Avalon. I need to ask about that; King Arthur disappeared into Avalon after being mortally wounded in a battle against his son. A boatful of female guardians escort him to the mysterious isle of glass, a place of hope as the "once" king will be "future" too. Neither tragedy nor death nor shattered hopes are the end of the story. There is always room for something new, whole, redeemed. Avalon, the glass island, offers healing and resurrection.

I call my place Glad River though, after a favorite novel of the same name—the book's author and I both inspired by the psalmist: "There is a river whose streams make glad the city of God." I am happier here than any other spot I have ever known. Sorrows and stress depart from my shoulders each time I drive onto the property.

—≡—

I am the son of immigrants, people who scrabbled hard to pay basic utility bills and buy groceries. We were never hungry but could not afford luxuries, not new clothes and certainly not second homes. We were unlike the affluent Canadians who looked down on us and threw us off their property, who wished we would return from whence we came.

When I was a child, our best family vacations were in rented cottages up north. For decades, I hoped for my own waterside haven, a seemingly impossible dream. Work as pastor and professor never paid much, and my social justice convictions could not justify a getaway residence. Yet whenever I neared water, I noticed each "For Sale" sign. On my way north to a meeting some years ago, I contacted a real estate agent on a whim. He showed me several properties and then this one with year-round insulation, good heating, tall windows, and river view. Afterward I spoke to my mother, and she generously offered an advance on my inheritance, quoting a Dutch proverb, "Better to give with warm hands than cold ones." Within weeks a long-held yearning was fulfilled.

Edward Abbey once claimed about a spot: "This is the most beautiful place on earth. There are many such places. Every man, every woman, carries in heart and mind, the image of the ideal place, the right place, the one true home."[*] I know where to find mine. In one of my earliest memories our family vacationed in Canadian Shield territory, the visit where James and his family decided against me. I marveled already then at boulders and bulky rocks, wind-bitten trees and light playing on waves. Ever since, I have loved this geography above all. I'm with Marjorie Kinnans Rawlings who writes: "I do not understand how anyone can live without some small place of enchantment to turn to."[**]

⸺

Canadians think of Muskoka, this stunning Canadian Shield region a couple of hours north of Toronto, as a haven for movie stars and NHL players with fancy mansions. Martin Short, Steven Spielberg, and Tom Hanks own holiday homes here, I'm told. Kurt Russell and Goldie Hawn's home reputedly has a human-constructed outdoor waterfall that can be turned on and off at will.

My place is in a scruffier, more modest end of the area. Rock formations are not as striking. Many people have lived on our road year-round for decades, primary not secondary homes. You have to travel plenty of kilometers to spot yachts or Jet Skis.

But still, this is my *second* residence, an extravagance—like that of the family of James, not Jim or Jimmy or Jamie. Roomier than many homes for

[*] Edward Abbey, *Desert Solitaire* (New York: Ballantine Books, 1968), 1.
[**] Marjorie Kinnan Rawlings, *Cross Creek* (New York: Simon & Schuster, 1942), 45.

large families that I have seen around the world, in North American inner cities and in Central American, Caribbean, and Middle Eastern countries that I have visited. No question that what I have here is a privilege, something unimaginable to my family a few decades ago. I savor the spot but feel guilt about justifying it.

I can afford it because of Pa's hard work and business success, a gift of his cold hands, another of his legacies. All that damned glass sold and spread over the decades now pays for something I always wanted—a beautiful location overlooking water, conducive to paddling and pondering and praying.

⇒⇐

When the real estate agent escorted me here the first time, one attractive feature he highlighted was its Muskoka Room. An old tradition around here puts "Muskoka" into names. Muskoka chairs for example. They look remarkably like what neighbors south of the border call Adirondack chairs. Not all cottages have Muskoka Rooms, but they are popular as they extend a cottage. These covered areas—porches or decks—with screens and perhaps windows let one sit partway outside, somewhat protected from wind or rain or, worst of all, bugs. Like immigrants, not entirely in one realm or the other. A place for relaxing, conversing, playing games, reading, staring into space.

Our Muskoka Room is entered from the kitchen through sliding glass patio doors, something else I admired in others' homes when I was a child. Its three walls jut from the front of the cottage and give a wide view to our front yard on the left, a forested lot to the right, the sky above, and the river ahead. The room is framed by cedar, its walls filled by a combination of acrylic glass and screens—in effect like a greenhouse or glass house. I can be out here for much of the year, in all kinds of weather. Unlike in Toronto, where I have long lists of things to do and where there is always noise, especially humming traffic, the Muskoka Room means stillness and relaxation: listening, reading, watching, breathing.

Its most impressive furniture is a table; its top is clear, thick glass, with aqua tinged edges. I keep worrying that something will drop on it and shatter it. Its base is an intricate weave of actual branches, still in their bark, a tribute to the many trees hereabouts.

An odd feature of the room are the windows. Within a few months of purchasing the cottage, a half dozen windows started cracking. No one could explain why, and my insurance company would not pay for the repairs. Happily, the damaging process soon stopped, but my view now includes small diagonal fractures. Nothing's perfect.

I retired early. My wife still works in the city and our adult children are married and live thousands of miles away in another country. I spend most of my time here alone, except for my beloved cat Fraser.

—————

Trees rise high all around, evergreen pine and cedar, maple and oak, crowding the shore. Because of thin soil, they do not get higher than forty or fifty feet. Banks are covered in vegetation with reeds, grass, ferns. The water reflects them all.

There is plenty to see: scampering squirrels and chipmunks; people paddling past in canoes or kayaks; Andy, my next-door neighbor, power swimming north against the current. I've watched snapping turtles bob in the eddies, minks and otters gambol along the river bank, beavers tote tree limbs through waves, a red-bellied sapsucker work over a trunk six feet from me. Muskrats skitter by on stones. Wild animals in natural settings, especially ones that do not want to be seen, that camouflage themselves and hide, remind me that some of life's best aspects are beyond my control.

One morning I heard an unimpressive squawk and turned to see a bald eagle slowly wielding its wingspan and floating upstream on air. Ospreys haunt these waters. Kingfishers stitch the air with hurtling bodies. Mallards, Canada geese, and loud ravens frequent this place, as do cormorants, buffleheads, red-breasted mergansers (often with babies), goldeneyes, and an occasional loon that reminds me of nearby lakes. I sometimes spy ruffed grouse pecking the earth, turkeys scrounging, American bittern imitating pointed reeds. A great blue heron—hunched like a bad-tempered old man—strides long-legged and angular through shallows with neck stretched and pointed bill poised to pierce fish or frog. If I move, it flees, usually with a resentful croak, unfurling broad wings and flapping majestically downstream.

A couple hundred yards upstream the river is deep and calm enough for diving and swimming, or paddle boats, but in front of our lot it encounters a rocky shoal across its forty-foot width. As leisurely moving water pours into our elbow's stony shallows, everything accelerates and the current tugs suddenly. Here the river seldom freezes entirely; water's too fast and unpredictable, leaves and branches spin counterintuitively, even seemingly upstream. When the cottage pipes freeze, I crawl gingerly over ice and lower buckets to get water that I must boil before using.

＝＝

In the room I listen to birds trill and shiver slightly at river-moistened air that feathers through the screen, tickling my face and neck, nudging and inviting me to savor the beauty, to feel peace, to have my heart mended. In early mornings, mist wisps hang and drift, smoking upward; the water warmer than air.

I usually get up before sunrise. Everything feels hushed and quiet, subdued and restrained. I go slow, read, sit still. At this time of day I most easily believe in God, most easily perceive God. Some time ago I went to bed discouraged, spending the night sleepless because of bad news that I'd heard late the evening before. But as the sun appeared I found everything outside quiet, peaceful, still, beautiful, the air clear and cool. Birds sang. I knew then that even in the worst circumstances, the world bespeaks beauty.

In the morning, the earth and I take long slow breaths before the day brings forth whatever the day will bring forth.

＝＝

Daydreaming comes easily here. My mind wanders beside water. I think, ponder, ruminate. Some of this is welcome, some not.

One summer, I obsessed about the previous work year, a tough one. My mind cycled back, rehearsing the antics of tyrannical bosses, bullies I now realize whose yelling and ultimatums and threats reminded me of the worst aspects of my father. I hoped that replaying griefs would gradually erase their power but fretted that perhaps I merely entrenched them.

Happily, my mind goes in other directions too. I lose myself in the sailing clouds, trees with leaves so densely green that it almost hurts my eyes, soothing water ripples, cool breezes along my neck, arms, and cheeks. In

The Wind in the Willows, Mole and Rat have a mystical experience while on the water. I get that.

A breeze drifts through the wooded lot next door, sifting through the screen and over the skin of my face and hands, bringing familiar greenhouse scents of peat and soil.

River reveries are nice when they arise. And they occur often here.

I embrace the view through all that glass.

PILGRIMAGE POSTSCRIPT

When I left my childhood denomination, I defied parents and pastors—and church elders confronting me in my parents' St. Davids living room—who predicted I would wander more. Hate to say it: they were right. My pilgrimage continued.

Within a week of joyously joining the Chapel, I moved away for university. At InterVarsity Christian Fellowship I got to know Christians of different denominations. I also for the first time read Roman Catholics (Dorothy Day, Daniel Berrigan, Thomas Merton, Hans Kung) who taught me much about faithful living and faithful Scripture reading. After university, I attended a Mennonite seminary and retreated regularly at a nearby Episcopal monastery, where years later I became an oblate. Easter vigils at the Basilica of Notre Dame left me in awe.

Lorna and I lived a summer in a Detroit Catholic Worker community. I was impressed by regular Eucharists amid service and protest. On Sundays she and I attended Church of the Messiah, an Episcopal church that blended Anglican liturgy with charismatic worship, all in the context of ministering to developmentally challenged members in an impoverished neighborhood.

We moved to inner city Chicago, idealistically hoping to make an impact, and wanted to worship where we lived. With no Mennonite church nearby, we went to the United Methodist Church around the corner. Other Mennonites attended too, service-oriented folks who, like us, walked to church. Still considering myself Mennonite, I was surprised to be asked to join the pastoral staff and pursue United Methodist ordination. I accepted the position, began work on an MDiv at a Presbyterian school, and entered discernment. I admired our local congregation and United Methodism, but theological studies reinforced my Anabaptism and I decided to accept a call to a Mennonite church.

I served two Mennonite congregations and continued my education, earning degrees at a Lutheran seminary and then a Baptist seminary. I was deeply influenced by getting to know Henri Nouwen. My closest pastoral colleagues were Baptists. I became friends with a Coptic Orthodox priest and worshiped occasionally with his congregation; he sometimes invited me to preach. I joined a Mennonite delegation to worship during Holy Week with Orthodox Christians in Syria. I grew more interested in liturgical theology, especially influenced by Robert Webber who was key in my doctor of ministry. I got involved with ecumenical projects sponsored by the Louisville Institute and Lilly Foundation. Eugene Peterson became my most significant mentor ever, although he would not let me call him that. He insisted I keep it simple, "friend."

I took theology seriously, treating it with rigor. A Mennonite colleague told me, "Arthur, your theology is Mennonite but you do it like a Dutch Calvinist." Mennonites are often ambivalent about theology; many boast of being "noncreedal." During my first seminary degree, I studied with the man who was history's most famous Mennonite theologian. He declined to call his work theology, though, preferring the term "ethics." Years later his theology is still a force to be reckoned with, but his personal ethics turned out to be atrocious.

I later taught at that Mennonite seminary. By then, given growing interest in liturgy (eloquent language, theologically grounded choreography, historical precedents) and love for sacraments, I called myself "Anglican Mennonite." The academic dean assigned Episcopalian students to me as an advisor. On Sundays, I longed for worship that was reverently God-oriented. I yearned for awe, wonder, mystery.

I accepted an endowed chair back in Canada at a "transdenominational" seminary. On our first weekend in Toronto, Lorna and I walked to the Anglican church nearest our new home. I've been connected there for over a dozen years now, longer than any other congregation. Within a couple years the diocese ordained me as a deacon and a year after that priested me. Since I had been ordained by Mennonites decades earlier, I called this a "refrocking." Eugene flew in from Montana to preach on that occasion.

Slipping along the spectrum, I now call myself a "Mennonite Anglican." I still hold to Mennonite ethics and admire Mennonite witness and service. I still subscribe to nonviolence, prioritizing community, honoring God's care for the poor and oppressed. And I also root myself in the worldwide church's "great traditions," particularly the creeds.

Anglicanism is in many ways a mess. I no longer look for a perfect church, seeking purity; I know I won't find it. Anglicanism is where I practice my faith and encourage others to practice theirs. It puts me in close fellowship with a broad range of believers, ones with whom I may disagree about many things, but who are all part of God's mysterious reign, invited to God's Welcome Table.

Many Anglican colleagues have the title "Father," just as beloved Henri did. Now some congregants call me that too. Jesus told us that we "have one Father, the one in heaven" and thus should call no one on earth our Father; I worry about his admonition sometimes. On the other hand, I no longer fret about living with paradox and contradictions.

ACKNOWLEDGMENTS

Completing a book always leaves me filled with immense gratitude to so many.

Above all, Lauren Winner, my senior MFA mentor, relentlessly prompted and prodded me toward something "wonderful and brave." More than once I was ready to give up; but Lauren helped me find my way forward.

Don Pape, my agent, reclaimed acquaintance and believed in this book. Karen Stiller cheered me on. Lisa Ann Cockrel, perspicacious editor, dedicated herself to helping me improve my work.

André Dubus III—great teaching chops at the Toronto Reference Library and then the Writing by Writers Manuscript Boot Camp—determined to help this find a place in the world.

More than anyone, Scott Russell Sanders first inspired me toward literary nonfiction and then taught me "Spiritual Writing and the Natural World" at the Glen Workshop in Santa Fe.

For decades Collegeville Institute—shout-out to Don Ottenhoff and Carla Durand—steadily urged me to grow as a writer. Through its graciousness, I worked at portions of this book with admired mentors: Robert Benson and Rebecca Youngblood at "Mapping the Geography of Grace" in Canton, Mississippi; Mary Potter Engel at "Writing Spirit, Writing Faith" on Whidbey Island; Donna Johnson at "The Art of Spiritual Memoir" in Austin, Texas; and dear Lauren again, this time "In the Thick of It" via Zoom.

Scott Cairns and the good Seattle Pacific MFA stewards helped me up my writing game—especially Paula Huston and Suzanne Antonetta.

The MFA program created a writers' community, including support and good counsel from Julie Lane-Gay, Amy Muia, Cat Ricketts, Sarah Sanderson. I am most significantly beholden to on-going workshopping partners, the Diviners: Sarah Orner, Janay Garrick, Anneliese Jolley.

And I'm grateful for other boon companions.

Kevin Abma has been a friend since I was twelve and witness to some of this book's claims. Glenn McCullough, John Rempel, Peter Roebbelen, and Yau Man Siew keep me grounded as I stumble toward faithfulness. Mike Vlasman makes me laugh and laughs at some of my jokes. Thank you to almost once-were-lost-but-now-are-found buddies John (Klassen and Longhurst) for conversations unlike any others I have ever had. Body-and-Soul kayakers—Dave Clark, Rudy Dirks, Ken Derksen, Ken Foster, Roy Foster, and Marv Franz—you are the men! For the first half of each year I look forward to our annual odyssey and then savor its memory for the next six months, beginning the cycle again in January.

John Suk, Irene Oudyk-Suk, Nick Overduin, and Nandy Heule, thank you for steadfast friendship.

Fr. Dean Mercer and the extraordinary clergy and parishioners of St. Paul's L'Amoreaux Anglican Church escort me to the Welcome Table. Fine folks at St. Philip's (Etobicoke), St. Thomas (Bracebridge), and Church of the Resurrection (East York) show support and affirmation.

Roelie Boers Vanderhout patiently answers many questions and encourages my writing, both emotionally and practically.

Fraser, the Phraser-Blade of Fraserburg, entertains and accompanies, especially beside Glad River.

No one does more for me as a writer and indeed in all of my life than my spouse, Lorna McDougall. Thank you, dear one, for honoring my call to write, and for sharing our hope that Erin and her Joseph, Paul and his Jennifer, always know how deeply they are loved.